Ponies, Patriots and Powder Monkeys:

A HISTORY OF CHILDREN IN AMERICA'S ARMED FORCES, 1776-1916

Eleanor C. Bishop

THE BISHOP PRESS

Library of Congress Catalog Card Number 82-73688

International Standard Book Number 0-911329-00-5

The Bishop Press, Del Mar, Calif. 92014

First Edition

Dedication

To my dear mother, Marceil Greenhalgh Bishop, whose encouragement, patience and understanding helped to make this book a reality.

Acknowledgments

I wish to credit the following persons and publishing houses for permission to quote from their publications:

From *David Glasgow Farragut* by Charles Lee Lewis. Copyright © 1941, U.S. Naval Institute, Annapolis, Maryland.

From *Surfboats and Horse Marines* by K. Jack Bauer. Copyright © 1959, U.S. Naval Institute, Annapolis, Maryland.

From "Destination Nowhere: Twilight of the Lightship" in U.S. Naval Institute *Proceedings,* March 1976. Copyright © 1976, U.S. Naval Institute, Annapolis, Maryland.

From *The Bravest Teenage Yanks* by Willard A. Heaps. Copyright © 1963. Duell, Sloan and Pearce, New York.

From *West Point* by Sidney Forman. Copyright © 1950. Columbia University Press, New York.

From *One Hundred Years at V.M.I.* by William Couper. Copyright © 1933. Michie Co., Charlottesville, Virginia.

From *The V.M.I. New Market Cadets* by William Couper. Copyright © 1939. Garrett & Massie, Richmond, Virginia.

From "Andrew Mealey and the Mongoose" in *The Marine Gazette,* Vol. 25, #4 February, 1931. Copyright © 1931. Marine Corps Association, Quantico, Virginia.

Table of Contents

Preface

This book was originally planned as a Bicentennial project, but time and other commitments closed in to make that goal an impossibility. Therefore, six years later, I still offer it as a contribution to American History in the hope that it will fill the void which exists regarding the role of America's children in her armed forces from its inception until just before World War I.

Many would argue that children have fought in America's twentieth century wars and I would agree that those still in their teens could be placed in that category. I am attempting to point out in this book that youngsters below seventeen served at all periods in the nation's history, but have not been adequately recognized. There have also been many instances of boys below legal age serving their country nobly. This book attempts to present the role of all our nation's youngsters who joined the services.

The idea for such a project came to me as a result of discovering the role played by two of my ancestors, one in colonial times and the other in the Civil War. Elnathan Hurd was an Ensign in No. 6 Connecticut Trained Band in 1717 at the age of seventeen. He was later made captain of his band, and fought in the French and Indian War and was wounded at Charlestown. By the time the Revolutionary War came he was seventy-four years old. Made Chairman of the "Committee of Safety" in the village of Newport, New Hampshire, he was captured and confined in Sugar House Prison in New York where he remained for six months before escaping and returning home.

His great-great-granddaughter married a man who had served as a drummer boy in the Civil War at the age of thirteen, Charles P. Dutchess. The thought came to me that if these two ancestors had served in the armed forces as youngsters, how many thousands more had done the same thing. The answer lies in this book.

I have used the nicknames of "Ponies," and "Powder Monkeys" interchangeably with Patriots—a term which applied to all the services.

Many people have contributed to the completion of this book, but I am particularly indebted to the following for their help and advice:

To Dr. Richard J. Sommers and Mr. Michael Winey, U.S. Army Military History Institute, Carlisle Barracks, Pennsylvania; Mr. Moreau Chambers, U.S. Army Center for Military History, Washington, D.C.; and Mrs. Regina Hanretta, U.S. Military Academy Archives, West Point, New York.

To: Ms. Janet Price, U.S. Naval Academy Archives and Ms. Pamela Evans, Nimitz Library, U.S. Naval Academy; Mrs. Agnes Hoover and Mr. Charles Haberlein, U.S. Naval Historical Center; and to Mrs. Patty Maddocks, U.S. Naval Institute, Annapolis, Maryland.

To: Captain J. E. Bennett, Jr., Mr. Charles Anthony Wood, and Mr. Richard Long of the U.S. Marine Corps Historical Center.

To: Mr. Robert Scheina and Mr. Truman Strobridge, past and present Historians, U.S. Coast Guard.

To: Mrs. Elaine Everly, Mr. William Heindahl and Mr. Jerry Hess, National Archives.

To: Mr. Donald Klosters and Dr. Harold D. Langley of

the Smithsonian Institution, and Mrs. Virginia Renner, Mrs. Doris Smedes and Mrs. Mary Wright, Henry E. Huntington Library, San Marino, California; Mrs. Georgia Hall, Clements Library, University of Michigan; and Mr. Richard B. Harrington, Curator, The Anne S. K. Brown Military Collection, Brown University. Mrs. Jean Johnson, New Hampshire Historical Society; Mrs. Janet Mills, Peabody Museum, Salem; Mr. W. T. Jordan, Jr., North Carolina Archives and History; and Lt. Colonel James E. Gaines, Jr., Head Librarian, and Mrs. Diane Jacobs, Curator, Virginia Military Institute; Mr. John Salmon, Virginia State Library.

To: Mr. Frederick Meigs, former Librarian, U.S. Navy Library; Staff Sergeant Mark Elrod formerly of the Military Music Collection, U.S.M.C. Historical Center; Mr. James Walker, Mr. Harry Schwartz and Mrs. Hope Holdcamper, former members of the National Archives.

Two gracious ladies shared family documents with me. Miss Elizabeth Koller loaned pictures of John Bailey, Marine Music Boy and Ms. Myrlee Marrett loaned a privately printed family history of Robert Henry Hendershot which provided new and interesting material on "The Drummer Boy of the Rappahannock".

Last, but not least, I owe a debt of gratitude to Dr. Ralph V. Patrick, Deputy Superintendent, San Diego City Schools; Mr. Brian Alexander, who edited the chapter on the U.S. Army; to Prof. Therese T. Whitcomb for her advice on the design, and most of all to my mother, my family, and many friends who contributed to its completion.

Introduction

Young boys from the ages of six to sixteen have served in the Armed Forces of the United States from its birth until as late as 1916. The less educated boys served as musicians in the U.S. Army and U.S. Marine Corps, as deckhands and cartridge carriers in the U.S. Navy and as wardroom and cabin boys in the U.S. Revenue Cutter Service. Educated boys became cadets and midshipmen, and many youngsters also served in the state volunteer units called to duty at times of war.

All the services eventually had very definite regulations regarding the enlistment of the boys, but the volunteer units tended to be less strict about the boys' ages. Since the Continental Army, Navy and Marines were for all practical purposes disbanded after the Revolutionary War, it was not until the formation of the War and Navy Departments in the 1790's that regulations were issued. During the Revolutionary period, therefore, the rules remained lax regarding the recruitment of minors in the services.

The U.S. Army program for youth was through enlistments in small numbers rather than indenture. The U.S. Navy and the U.S. Marine Corps both had apprentice programs and the U.S. Revenue Cutter Service allowed young boys of thirteen to enlist in the service. The other seafaring services, the U.S. Coast Survey, the Lighthouse Service, and the Life Saving Service also admitted young boys.

Little is known about the enlistment of boys in the Continental Forces. In many cases, these children were sons of commanding officers of units in the Army, or captains of ships in the Navy. Because of the desperate times that faced the colonists, every man available could find a regiment or ship that needed him. Americans were inexperienced in the art of warfare on a grand scale; the Mother Country had provided the troops and ships to defend the colonies in the past, notably during the French and Indian War. Americans' experience in warfare had been limited to service in a colonial militia or on board a privateer.

The best known and most romanticized youth in the armed forces has been the drummer boy. From Revolutionary times, he took his place as a symbol of the patriotic spirit of the American people. We find the drummer boy in several well-known paintings of different wars, particularly Archibald M. Willard's "The Spirit of '76" and Winslow Homer's paintings of the Civil War. The fifer and later the bugler have also symbolized the call to arms for American patriots whether it was 1776, 1846, or 1917.

When we think of drummers and fifers, we tend to picture the citizen soldiers who rushed to the aid of their country in time of need. But what of the years between the wars; who served as drummers and fifers and who manned the ships during those periods? We shall see that there was a regular program in each service to perform those roles. Citizen and professional alike tell the story of America's children in the armed forces.

Their contributions have been neglected to a large extent. Hopefully, this book will place them in their proper perspective and illustrate the active and important part they played in the history of our country in war and peace.

CHAPTER 1

ARMY

When the Declaration of Independence was signed on July 4, 1776, the United States of America became a reality, but with that reality came the responsibility of raising an army. The new nation was born of paper, but it would have to be baptized in blood. The duty of recruiting and training the new army fell variously upon the shoulders of the states, the Continental Congress and George Washington. Predictably, the process was highly disorganized.

I. Drummers and Fifers 1776-1861

Because of the confusion at the start of the Revolutionary War, it was very easy for young boys to join up with their local units. No age requirements had to be met, and because the boys were used mostly as drummers, fifers and guards, roles that presumed a more organized fighting force, the only regulations regarding their duties concerned uniforms. Since the drummers and fifers were meant to direct the movements of troops on the battlefield, it immediately became obvious that they would have to be readily distinguishable from the rest of the force so they could be easily located by the commanding officer. For this reason, Washington issued orders that the musicians should be dressed differently from their comrades. Usually this meant a reversing of colors. If, for example, the troops had blue uniforms with buff facings and linings, the drummers and fifers had buff (possibly white) uniforms with blue facings and linings. Even if a unit was too poor to have the regulation uniform (each unit was responsible for its own purchase of equipment) and wore hunting shirts and breeches, the drummers wore a special shirt with dark cuffs.

The next year, 1777, saw the appearance of *Von Steuben's Regulations for the Order and Discipline of the Troops of the United States,* and firmer rules began to take hold. Rather than leaving practice time up to the drum major or the commanding officer, a regular schedule was established. At Germantown, Pennsylvania, for example, the musicians were to practice at least four hours per day, and at Valley Forge the hour of 6:00 to 7:00 a.m. was reserved for rehearsal. Some drummers, undaunted by the severe conditions at Valley Forge, practiced on their own time, even to the point of confusing the troops. At Springfield, Virginia, musicians were required to pay the fife or drum major five shillings per month until such time as they were able to assume their duties and take care of their own instruments. They also had to pay for any instrument that was damaged or destroyed. This often consumed a large portion of the $7.33 they were paid.

Except for those caught in extreme hardship areas, life for the youngsters in the army during the Revolutionary War does not seem to have been much more severe than their lives as civilians. Most of the boys were from rural areas and were quite used to the rigors of farm life. Exactly why the boys joined and the reasons for their parents allowing them is unclear, but each seems to have had his own reasons. Many boys went in search of excitement. Many parents allowed their sons to go to be with their fathers or because their fathers were unable to serve. In many ways, the Revolution was a part-time affair and it was felt that a son could join in place of his father, who had to tend to the farming, and return for planting or harvesting.

One such boy was Daniel Granger who joined the Continental Army in December of 1775 at the age of thirteen. During this first stint in the army, Granger served mainly as a guard:

> Here I did duty as a soldier three months mounted guard several times. The first time that I was detached was on the main guard and I prepared my breakfast the night before so as to be ready, at the call of the little bell, and not to get a caning from him (the sergeant) for negligence as some others did.[1]

After a year of watching the wood and stores and later the British prisoners, including one his own age, the son of a British officer, Granger returned to help with the harvest, and, in August of that year enlisted still another time to serve as a musician. It was during this tour that Granger witnessed the surrender of Burgoyne, the seige of Boston, and the controversy over Benedict Arnold's betrayal of West Point. After one more trip back to the farm, Granger entered the service for the last time in 1780 to serve as a drummer, a position he held until the end of the war. As Granger's case illustrates, few children, if any, actually took part in the fighting. Although legend has long surrounded the role Andrew Jackson played in the fighting in South Carolina, he asserts that he saw little action as a teenager:

> I was never regularly enlisted, being only fourteen when the war practically ended. When I took the field it was with Colonel Davie who never put me in the ranks, but used me as a mounted orderly or messenger...the only weapons I had were a pistol that Colonel Davie gave me and a small fowling piece that my Uncle Crawford lent to me.[2]

Andrew Jackson is famed for an incident which occurred

after his capture following the skirmish at Captain Sand's house (Sand was a neighbor of Jackson's):

> A lieutenant of Tarleton's Light Dragoons tried to make me clean his boots and cut my arm with his saber when I refused. After that, they kept me in jail at Camden about two months, starved me nearly to death and gave me the smallpox.[3]

Jackson's brother Robert, who was captured at the same time, eventually died of smallpox as did his mother who had arranged for his release from the British.

Still, even though the boys' chances of being killed were much smaller than those of the regular troops, they always faced the possibility of injury or capture. Ebenezer Fletcher was one such boy. He relates the following about his captivity:

> An old negro came and took my fife, which I considered as the greatest insult I had received while with the enemy. The Indians often came and abused me with their language, calling us Yankees and rebels; but they were not allowed to injure us. I was stripped of everything valuable about me.[4]

It is interesting to note that the youngest drummer boy to have served in the Revolution was Nathan Futrell, age seven. The most important, if such a label can be used, was probably Sergeant John George who served with Washington at Brandywine, Germantown, Monmouth, Valley Forge and finally, Yorktown. He was sixteen years old when he became Washington's drummer.

After the Revolutionary War, the Continental Army was disbanded. When the War Department was established in 1789, more rules were adopted which brought order to the enlistment process. The Army Regulations of 1802 stated that no person under the age of twenty-one should be enlisted without the consent of his parent, guardian or master but it did not specify any minimum entrance age when a boy did have consent.

New regulations in 1813 seemed to clarify the minimum age by specifying that "healthy, active" boys between the ages of 14 and 18 could be enlisted as musicians with parental consent. After the War of 1812, however, a rash of incidents took place over the enlistment of minors which brought a flurry of protest from the newly formed Peace Establishment, as the new Army was then being termed. As a result, the Secretary of War issued orders in 1815 that all apprentices and minors who had enlisted without the consent of their parents, masters or guardians would be discharged upon application. When Lieutenant Colonel Clinch of the Fourth Infantry claimed that half of the men of his unit wanted to be discharged on the ground of their minority, he would discharge each one accordingly, although he believed that he was being duped. Lacking the enlistment papers, he was forced to release those asking for a discharge.

Many men got writs of habeas corpus, and Colonel Clinch was required to report the proceedings before the civil courts of his district. The judge was discharging men on the grounds of minority or enlistment for the war. If the War Department could prove by enlistment papers that they were minors enlisting with the consent of their parents, they remained in the Army. The Secretary of War finally directed that all minors be promptly discharged on application for that purpose.

An order from the Adjutant and Inspector General's Office on February 18, 1820 established a penalty for officers who enlisted "...minors who are discharged by the civil authority for want of a written consent of parents or guardians...." Those who were penalized were forced to pay "the bounty and other expenses" incurred by the army when the boy was signed up. That same order prohibited "...the enlistment of any negro or mulatto" into the armed forces. This, despite the fact that such negroes as drummer boy Jordan B. Noble, who fought with Andrew Jackson at New Orleans, had distinguished themselves in battle.

In the years following the War of Independence and the War of 1812, America began moving westward at a faster rate and the Army began enlisting more and more young musicians who were hungry for the adventure of life beyond the farm or the newly industrialized city. Most of these youngsters were from the lower economic strata and some were victims of poverty. Others were orphans or had lost one of their parents. The Army provided a refuge, and in spite of the 1802 and 1820 regulations, it took in youngsters of all ages and colors. Boys served as fifers and drummers in the infantry and heavy artillery and as buglers in the cavalry and light artillery. Many boys, both regular Army and volunteers, served in the Mexican War (including John Rouse, a black drummer boy who lost part of his left arm in 1836 at Vera Cruz) and in confrontations with American Indians.

The best description of what life was like for a youngster in the Army during this period comes from Augustus Meyers' book *Ten Years in the Ranks, U.S. Army.* Meyers, a New Yorker, was typical of many boys of the period. His father had died and his widowed mother felt that Augustus would find security in the Army. For this reason, twelve year old Augustus entered the Army on March 31, 1854 for a period of five years.

When Meyers crossed over to Governor's Island in New York where the boys learning music were stationed, he discovered that his living quarters consisted of six iron double bedsteads with a bedsack stuffed with straw laying on top. There were no sheets or pillows, but Meyers was given two blankets. A coal fire and his practice of sleeping in longjohns assured that he would be kept warm. In the morning, Meyers was awakened with the sounds of "Reveille". Then he went outside to pump himself a basin full of water, a practice which became unbearable and sometimes impossible in frigid winter temperatures.

After washing, Meyers was treated to a breakfast of a piece of cold boiled salt pork, a piece of bread and a large bowl of coffee after which he made his bed, polished the brass buttons on his uniform and chalked the white braid on his jacket. His uniform required quite a bit of attention because it was so ornate. The single breasted overcoat had a cape reaching down to the elbows with a row of brass buttons on the breast and the cape with still more buttons on the coat tails. The jacket came to his hips and was equipped with an inside breast pocket, a row of brass buttons down the front and some on the sleeves. His cap, called a forage or fatigue cap, had a large overhanging crown with a welt of thick dark blue cloth, a chinstrap with one brass button on each side, and a leather visor. A strip of stiff, black shoe leather about two and one-half inches wide, which the boys called a "dog collar", served as a cravat to keep Meyers' head elevated. So much importance was given to the uniform that most of Meyers' eight dollars a month pay went for tailoring and laundering expenses.

At eight a.m., Meyers fell in for guard mounting and returned to the South Battery for school at nine. After two hours of reading, writing and arithmetic, he practiced on his fife with the other twenty-four "straw blowers" (fifers), while the drummers or "sheepskin fiddlers" (drummers) went outside and beat a resounding chorus that could be heard all the way to Brooklyn. If Meyers was lucky, he would practice well enough on his chosen instrument that his tobacco-chewing instructor would not be tempted to demonstrate proper technique and leave behind bits of tobacco and its accompanying odor. Unfortunately, Meyers' fife had to be washed with soap and water many times.

Meyers' dinner, which was served at noon, consisted mainly of a bowl of rice soup, a piece of boiled beef and bread. After dinner, Meyers was free to do as he liked until two when school resumed.

At four, Meyers found himself answering the drums calling "assembly" and rushing for the parade ground. Since he was a fifer, he stood on the right and answered roll call after which "break ranks" was beaten out and it was time for a supper of stewed diced apples, black coffee and a four-ounce slice of bread. Meyers then returned to his quarters for an evening of reading by tallow candlelight or playing a game such as checkers. That lasted until nine when "Tattoo" was played and all the boys went to sleep (Taps was not composed until the Civil War).

Saturday and Sunday were a welcome relief to Meyers because his only duties were the scrubbing of floors and benches on Saturday afternoon. On Sunday, guard mounting at eight was followed by a church service at ten thirty which Meyers found boring. To pass the time, he read the commemorative plaques on the pews, one being in memory of the soldiers and music boys who were lost at sea aboard the *San Francisco* on its way to California. Late Sunday afternoon, however, dress parade took place and the smart musician would have his uniform and instrument in perfect order, especially on the bi-monthly general inspection days. They were held just before payday and the disheveled soldier could be penalized.

Musicians' pay was one dollar more a month than that of a private, so at the end of two months, Augustus received sixteen dollars. Sutlers', tailors' and laundresses' bills were deducted, leaving him with just a few dollars. Luckily, Congress raised the musician's pay to $12.00 a month soon thereafter.

The boys could be punished for a variety of offenses, the most common of which was gambling. Although gambling was forbidden, the boys hid in different places on the island, playing cards and dice. Punishment varied according to the offense. If the offense was minor, the judgment usually included a few whacks over the shoulder with a rattan by a noncom, confinement to quarters and/or deprivation of passes to New York. More serious offenders were sentenced to "walk the ring", a circular path about 30 feet in diameter. Meyers would soon witness much more severe punishment.

Ten months after arriving on Governor's Island, Meyers received his first duty assignment and set out for Carlisle Barracks, Pennsylvania, where he joined Company D of the Second U.S. Infantry. At first, life appeared to be much more pleasant at Carlisle; the food was better and included fresh fruit and milk from neighboring farms. The music boys patronized a small ice cream and candy store when they went into town, and wore their best uniforms with a red sash to replace the belt and sword they wore on post.

Meyers was awakened to the reality of regular army life when he was forced to take part in a drumming out of two soldiers who had been found guilty of desertion. After their conviction, the men had had their heads shaved and the letter "D" branded on their hips. Then they were subjected to the humiliation of being drummed out of the service. All the troops in the camp were drawn up on the parade ground for the ritual as the fifers and drummers, including Meyers, marched to the guard house. Here the musicians formed ranks through which the prisoners were marched in front of four privates and a corporal with fixed bayonets. They strode to the parade ground to the tune of "The Rogue's March". The two deserters were marched past the ranks of companies around all four sides of the parade ground. Then it was back to the guardhouse and the gate to the camp. There, the prisoners received their hats and bundles containing dishonorable discharges and were sent down the road towards town. In an apparent attempt to avoid further embarrassment, the two bypassed the road by running across a field.

Although there was more pressure and formality at Carlisle than at Governor's Island, Meyers did find time for levity. He would sometimes find his fife stuffed with paper or rags and he soon realized the importance of inspecting his instrument before a parade. In retaliation, he would loosen the snares on a fellow musician's drumhead or grease the skin. Still, the duty was more demanding since he had to attend four roll calls per day, practice his fife and serve as an orderly at the adjutant's office about once a week.

It was with mixed emotions that Meyers left Carlisle for Fort Pierre on the Missouri River in the Nebraska Territory (now Pierre, South Dakota). The Second Infantry had received orders in June of 1855 and Meyers immediately began to look forward to new adventures in what was still largely a wilderness area; the prospects of life with the Indians excited him.

The troops marched to the Carlisle station with refrains of "The Girl I Left Behind Me" and "The Bold Soldier Boy" ringing in their ears. Their haversacks had been stuffed with a three-day ration of hard bread and boiled salt pork. When the train arrived, the enlisted men took their seats on uncomfortable wooden benches in the "immigrant cars". This would be their home during the trip from Pennsylvania, through Ohio and Indiana to Alton, Illinois, where they were moved into barns to await the arrival of the steamboat which would take them down to the junction of the Mississippi and the Missouri Rivers. Predictably, Meyers enjoyed this part of the trip the most. He had only to blow three roll calls a day and then was free to observe the new world around him; his observations of life on the Mississippi are well recorded in his book and give a vivid description of the area before the Civil War.

Meyers' Second Infantry stopped off at an old, dilapidated frontier post called Fort Leavenworth in Kansas for a three-week stay. When they arrived, cholera was raging and soon the disease took the lives of four soldiers in Company A of the Second Infantry. Since Leavenworth had no musicians of its own, Meyers and his drummer were ordered to play the "Dead March" at all the funerals. The two were kept busy. As the disease raged on, they played a funeral every morning, plus some in the afternoon and evening, for the entire three weeks. These funerals usually consisted of Bible readings, three volleys from the rifles and Meyers' fife and drum music.

The three weeks of funerals finally ended when Company D boarded a boat which would take them from Leavenworth to St. Joseph, Missouri, and, finally, their destination of St. Pierre, Nebraska Territory about 1500 miles north of St. Louis. During his year long stay, Meyers experienced the coldest winter of his young life. The temperature was often far below freezing and the substandard housing made matters even worse. Much of this hardship was offset, in Meyers' mind at least, by his contacts with the Sioux Indians. He became so intimately acquainted with them that he was able to learn their complex language.

Company D moved from fort to fort in the territory during the next several years. In 1857, Augustus Meyers was court martialed, at age fifteen, for refusing to take his turn at beating a prisoner. Meyers, who had demonstrated a strong distaste for aiding in the punishment of fellow soldiers back at the Carlisle drumming out ceremony, would now be punished himself. After his conviction, he was sentenced to the guardhouse for thirty days, ten in solitary confinement, a diet of bread and water, a forfeiture of a month's pay and hard labor. Fortunately for Meyers, he found he was popular with the guards. They took him out of his cell and into the guardroom at night and often smuggled food to him. Friends even managed to get candies and books into his cell.

When Meyers' enlistment was up in March of 1859, he collected his clothing allowance, the mileage to New York and $2.00 per month which the Army had saved for him, $30.00 in all, and returned to New York only to reenlist after one year as a civilian. Meyers was eighteen in March of 1860. He reenlisted for five more years, not knowing he was about to be part of America's War of the Rebellion.

II. Cadets & Music Boys at West Point 1802-1872

The U.S. Military Academy, founded in 1802, enrolled young boys from the higher socio-economic groups who entered the academy at a young age. A list of the classes at West Point in 1819 shows that some cadets were twelve years old. The superintendent was authorized to appoint as many cadets as needed to academic positions. He was authorized to pay them $10.00 and the appointment was considered an honor.

Henry Brewerton, age twelve, a second classman in 1819, was also acting assistant teacher of drawing. His classmate, Thomas Sudler, fourteen, was an acting assistant and professor of mathematics. Joseph Mansfield, '22, fourteen years old, served as acting assistant professor of philosophy; Alfred Mordecai, '22, fifteen years old, was an acting assistant professor of mathematics.

A vivid description of the youthfulness of the cadets is found in a letter written by William Davidson Frazer, U.S.M.A., Class of 1834, to Reverend James P. Wilson:

> When at first us new Cadets stood post the old cadets used to come round at night and try to fool us in trying to cross our post, and to frighten us at night, but some of our fellows run at some of them and came very near running some through. Immediately after guard mounting we had Artillery drill, we had six large brass field pieces, at first it used to almost deafen me, it would have astonished you I think to see little boys not 4 ft. high touching off a large cannon, and performing all the different duties necessary to man a piece.[6]

The curriculum was considered on a par with the better high schools of the East but far behind Harvard, Yale and Princeton. Trigonometry, algebra, geometry and French were included in the first year course; the second year included calculus, surveying, geography, English grammar, topography and drawing. In addition, the cadets were taught the rudiments of artillery, infantry and cavalry practice, but not strategy. When America's most famous future generals were cadets it is said that West Point turned out good tacticians and narrow specialists.

Life at the academy during these years was not a great deal better than Meyers' on Governor's Island. At first, the rooms were bare and supplied only with a mattress on the floor. Later, beds and chairs were added. The boys were paid more, twenty-eight dollars per month, but they also had to buy their own food and clothing. While, on the whole, the regulations were the same, the cadets were forbidden to possess a dog or horse, use tobacco (something the Governor's Island boys did regularly), or receive money or goods from home. If found guilty of any of these offenses or of failing to keep one's room or uniform (which consisted of a stiff grey coat, standing collar, tight white pants and a cap of black felt with a rounded crown and black pompon) in perfect order, demerits were issued. Two hundred demerits in one year resulted in dismissal. A cadet could be dismissed immediately for insulting a sentinel, playing cards, misbehaving in chapel, possessing liquor or duelling. Predictably, they were expected to become experts at marching, standing guard, and handling weapons. As future officers and gentlemen, they were also expected to become excellent dancers.

The cadets awakened at dawn to attend roll call, studied mathematics, cleaned their rooms and weapons until breakfast at seven. Their breakfast consisted of bread and butter and meat. After guard mount at eight, they attended class until eleven reciting in mathematics. Eleven until one was reserved for French. After dinner at one, the cadets recited in French until four. From that time until sunset, the cadets had military exercises and dress parade. After supper, mathematics was again studied until nine-thirty; tattoo was blown at ten (taps after the Civil War).

West Point produced many officers who became famous generals in the history of our country and several of them entered the Military Academy at an early age. They were to receive their "baptism of fire" in the Mexican War and achieve fame in the Civil War where they would be tested severely.

On the Union side, George B. McClellan (appointed by President Andrew Jackson) and George G. Meade both entered at the age of fifteen and a half; the former in the Class of 1846, the latter in the Class of 1835. Sherman and Sheridan both entered as sixteen-year olds; Sherman graduated in 1840, and Sheridan after a year's suspension (for fighting) graduated with the Class of 1853.

The Confederates claimed Pierre Gustave Toutant

Beauregard and Braxton Bragg, both Southern lads who entered at the age of sixteen and graduated a year apart; Bragg in 1837 and Beauregard in 1838.

The early age at which these boys entered West Point was not a hindrance to their success at the Academy. Beauregard graduated second in his class, Bragg fifth; Meade nineteenth, McClellan second and Sherman sixth. Even with Sheridan's bad luck, he managed to graduate thirty-second out of a class of fifty-two.

Along with the sixteen and under future generals, James Abbot McNeill Whistler entered West Point in 1841 at the age of sixteen and a half and remained three years. He stood at the head of his class in drawing, but failed chemistry which forced him to retire to a life which brought him fame as one of America's greatest artists after a stint with the U.S. Coast Survey.

In the early 1840's, there were also music boys who formed the Field Music Section of the U.S. Military Academy Band. Colonel Richard Delafield, Superintendent of the Academy, approved the addition of six fifers and six drummers to be attached to the band as "boys learning music." This was common in the Marine Corps and in the rest of the Army, with the latter group being trained at Governor's Island.

This practice lasted well into the Civil War, but the age was not as low as it had been in the 1840's. After 1866, the Military Academy Band was decreased in size and it became the practice for teenage sons or relatives of band members to join it as "boys in training" until an authorized vacancy occurred. The entire practice was frowned upon by the War Department, although it had originally given its approval to Colonel Delafield's plan. He had patterned the idea after the program at Governor's Island, which was described in detail earlier in the section about Augustus Meyers.

III. Cadets of the Confederacy

The duties of midshipmen dictated that they experience actual battle, wounds and death because they were part of the fleet from its inception until the establishment of the U.S. Naval Academy in 1845. The cadets, however, remained secure from the dangers of war.

There were three exceptions to cadets' lack of experience in combat and to include them will probably question their role as patriots. The Civil War forced the cadets of the two best known military academies of the South, the Virginia Military Institute and the South Carolina Military Academy, and the lesser known University of Alabama Cadet Corps, to show their loyalty to their home state rather than to the nation. However, they were youngsters, inspired by their officers and the decision for combat was declared by their superiors. They fought bravely and added their names to the list of brave children whose names are on the honor roll.

A. Virginia Military Institute

VMI, founded in 1839, was "created for the purpose of providing a liberal education, coupled with a military training in the belief that its graduates would prove valuable citizens all the more useful because of being capable of bearing arms efficiently in the hour of their country's need." The idea was to have cadets instead of soldiers guard the state's muskets at the arsenal located in Lexington and to experience an interchange with the students of nearby Washington College.

Boys were admitted to the college between the ages of fourteen and eighteen. The first class had twenty-eight cadets, twenty of them "state cadets" representing senatorial districts who received no pay for guarding the state's muskets but received the education instead. Eight others were known as "irregular" cadets because they paid all their expenses.

The cadet uniform consisted of a "light gray cloth

coatee," single breasted with one row of eight gilt convex buttons in front, impressed with the arms of the State of Virginia. The cap was black leather, a bell crowned seven inches high with a visor of leather in front, slightly polished, a diamond-shaped yellow plate in front with the arms of the State of Virginia impressed and a white pompon six inches long.

The first graduating class provided the country with officers to fight in the Mexican War in 1846. By 1851, there were one hunded and seventeen cadets and by the opening of hostilities in the Civil War the enrollment had doubled.

Before the war began, cadets dressed in red flannel shirts were present at the execution of John Brown at Charlestown on December 2, 1859. Governor Wise of Virginia had ordered a portion of the military of the state to be present, and in the military force were sixty-four cadets of infantry and twenty-one artillerists under the command of Major Thomas Jonathan Jackson, professor of natural and experimental philosophy and professor of artillery. The VMI contingent stood immediately in the rear of the gallows, the prelude to the many deaths the cadets would witness during the War of the Rebellion.

When the war came, the governor of Virginia stated that the Corps of Cadets was part of the state's defense forces, but circumstances dictated that the cadets would take part in offensive actions and suffer loss of life and limb. On April 21, 1861, Jackson took the greater part of the Corps to Richmond to drill the Confederate troops and the remaining cadets stayed in Lexington to guard the arsenal.

In the spring of 1862, their former professor, now the famous General "Stonewall" Jackson, requested that the cadets be part of his expedition into the Shenandoah Valley. Commandant Smith agreed, but the Board of Visitors questioned the propriety of such an action; the cadets went with Jackson in what became known as the McDowell Campaign, and did not suffer any casualties, but experienced many hardships.

The cadets met their baptism of blood and achieved fame

at New Market, Virginia, May 12, 1864. The Union general, Franz Sigel marched up the Shenandoah Valley from Winchester to New Market hoping to reach Staunton and cut the Virginia Central Railroad. Confederate General J. D. Imboden commanded the only Confederate forces in the Valley at the time and he notified the VMI Superintendent to have the Corps of Cadets ready to reinforce his small army of 1,500 consisting of cavalry, mounted infantry and a battery of six guns. Since the valley was part of the Virginia department, General John C. Breckinridge assumed command of the Confederate forces for the defense of the valley and ordered the Corps of Cadets to join him at Staunton.

The cadets left for Staunton on May 11th and marched eighteen miles to Midway, where they spent the night sleeping in the rain. The next day, they marched eighteen miles to Staunton. On the 13th, the Corps joined Breckinridge's troops and marched eighteen more miles to Valley Pike, and the following day, fifteen miles to within seven miles of New Market where they went into camp to await action.

On Sunday, the fifteenth, the cadets took to the battlefield and formed into a line of battle. A heavy artillery siege caught them in an orchard:

> They were going up in perfect line, the colors a little in advance. The battery of four pieces, was pouring canister into them and two color-bearers were knocked down. When within four hundred yards, the infantry rose and opened upon them. While doing this, Major Ship was knocked down by a piece of shell, and lay for a moment breathless, but almost was on his feet, and calling out to the cadets, 'Follow my lead, boys!' started for the artillery, and which they captured, together with a large part of the infantry, who said they felt shamed that they had been whipped by boys.[6]

Then the Corps charged:

> So eager were the cadets to charge the enemy, 100

> to 150 yards off, that it was difficult for them to find time to load and shoot their old-fashioned muzzle loading muskets. This, the final charge, commenced in the wheat field, then a field of mud, just north of the Bushong orchard, and continued for some distance north toward the Pike bridge over the Shenandoah.[7]

The cadets continued to pursue the retreating army until General Breckinridge gave the order for them to halt.

Two hundred forty-seven cadets took part in the Battle of New Market; ten were killed or died of wounds and forty-five were wounded. Eighteen of the boys in the battle were only fifteen; seven were sixteen.

B. South Carolina Military Academy

In 1833, the South Carolina legislature established two arsenals and magazines, one at Charleston, the other at Columbia. From these two sites, the South Carolina Military Academy was formed and cadets from both distinguished themselves in the Civil War.

Following the example of the Virginia Military Institute, it was felt that the young men of South Carolina should have an opportunity for a liberal arts education, with military discipline and preparation. In 1841, the Arsenal at Columbia was converted to a military school by the governor over the objections of the legislature. He dismissed the soldiers and enlisted boys from the several districts of the state selected by the Commissioners of the Poor.

The year 1842 marks the official birthday of the Citadel and by 1843, both the Citadel and Arsenal academies began their sessions with both beneficiary cadets and pay cadets. The beneficiary cadets took the place of the soldiers who had served as guards at the Citadel and the Arsenal and were maintained at public expense. The pay cadets were charged $200.00 a year. Candidates for admission ranged in age from fifteen to nineteen years. The first year was spent at the Arsenal, the remaining three at the Citadel.

The first class graduated in 1846 at the beginning of the Mexican War and the cadets acted as drillmasters for the Palmetto Regiment which represented South Carolina in the war. A boy of sixteen by the name of Allen H. Little, served in the Palmetto Regiment and lost an arm in the war. Upon his return home, he was awarded a scholarship to the State Military Academies. He spent two years completing the courses at the Arsenal, but stood at the head of his class for his last two years and graduated first in 1852 at the Citadel. He had hoped to be a lawyer, but took sick and was dead within the year.

When South Carolina seceded from the Union, the status of the Arsenal and Citadel changed from places of education to military posts. The legislature passed an act on January 28, 1861, stating that officers and students of the Citadel and Arsenal "shall constitute a military corps entitled 'The Battalion of State Cadets'."

The cadets played both defensive and offensive roles in the war. After Port Royal fell in November, 1861, the cadets supported the Washington Artillery at Wappoo Cut. There was concern that gunboats from Port Royal would try to take Charleston through the inland route, but when the danger appeared over, the cadets resumed their academic pursuits until June of 1862.

Then the order came for the cadets to guard James Island and mount heavy guns there. There was a conflict in orders between General James Jones, the Chairman of the Board of Visitors and General John C. Pemberton. The former wanted the cadets back to the Academy, and the latter wanted them to remain on the island. Upon the advice of the Chief Ordnance Officer, Lt. Colonel Wagner, Pemberton decided to follow Jones' recommendation.

This action had far reaching effects because thirty-six cadets deserted and formed what was later known as the Cadet Company, a cavalry unit which performed gallantly in the war. Because many felt Charleston was in danger, the cadets should have remained on James Island; many cadets asked to withdraw, but were persuaded that the

state needed them at this critical time.

The cadets had occasional tours of guard duty in different parts of Charleston until July 10, 1863, when the Union troops captured the upper end of Morris Island. It was again thought the cadets would be needed for the defense of the batteries there, and again they were disappointed and were joined by the Arsenal Cadets for a short period of time.

Finally in June of 1864, the cadets returned to James Island and remained there until fall when they were ordered into camp at Orangeburg due to the yellow fever raging in Charleston. Finally in December, they were ordered back to Charleston to defend the Charleston and Savannah Railroad.

Their first moment of glory came on December 6th and 7th at the Battle of Tulifinny. Broad River, the wide extension of Port Royal Sound, comes to a head in three tidal rivers, the Coosawatchie, Tulifinny and Pocotaglio Rivers. The Charleston and Savannah Railroad crosses these rivers and it was the railroad which was the objective of the Federal troops at Tulifinny.

Major J. B. White, Commander of the Battalion of States Cadets, was ordered by the Adjutant and Inspector General of South Carolina, to report to the nearest Confederate general for service in the field. Orders were changed by the governor, and Major White went to Charleston where the Arsenal Corps under Captain J. P. Thomas reported to White. The Citadel Corps formed Company A; the Arsenal formed Cadet Company B.

December 3, 1864, the battalion was ordered to the Coosawatchie, but stopped at the Pocotaglio. Three days later, the Federal forces threatened the railway and the battalion went to protect the Tulifinny trestle, but were then ordered to attack the enemy who was fighting the Confederates in front. Pushed, the cadets returned to their position on the railroad.

On December 7th, Major White took Company A and other Confederate troops on a scouting expedition to determine the enemy's position with the idea of a future attack. White's troops became engaged with an attack by the enemy, but drove them back to their entrenchments and then retreated.

This three hour skirmish depleted the ammunition supply of Company A, and Company B relieved their beleaguered companions. The behavior of the cadets won high praise from the commanding general and every cadet acted with gallantry. One cadet was killed and six were wounded.

George M. Coffin of the Arsenal Academy, a fourth classman, relates being sent to Charleston to join the Citadel cadets (first, second, and third year classmen) to form the battalion; and the subsequent encounter with the Federals at Tulifinny:

> The Arsenal Company was held in reserve. We lay down to avoid the bullets and shells passing over us, and in a heavy rain on some swampy ground. We were, after an hour or so, sent in on the firing line to relieve the Citadel Company which had suffered considerable casualties. . . . Our company stayed in a while firing at the Yanks, though I did not see any. We had muzzle-loading, Springfield rifles, and after each shot had to tear cartridge, run down bullet, restore ramrod and put on percussion cap before we could fire again. The enemy must have been driven back by the Citadel Company, because after awhile we were withdrawn to some rifle pits in an open field. There we stayed until night, when we were relieved and went into camp with fires to warm us and dry our wet clothes.[8]

The Cadet Company was formed in the spring of 1862 by cadets disillusioned by Pemberton's decision to send the cadets back to the Citadel rather than continue guarding James Island. Five first classmen, eleven second classmen and twenty third classmen, left the Citadel and were joined by fourth classmen from the Arsenal and other friends. Although unauthorized to take such action, the Cadet Company became part of the Sixth Regiment of the

South Carolina Cavalry.

The regiment was composed of mostly recruits and the cadets were capable of drilling any size military unit. Colonel Hugh Aiken, the commander of the regiment, detailed the officers of the cadet company to form a school for the officers and non-commissioned officers to instruct them in Hardee's Tactics.

When the regiment went to Virginia in the spring of 1864, it was considered the finest equipped regiment of South Carolina due in no small part to the efficiency and ability of the cadet officers. Prior to the regiment's departure for the North, the Cadet Company supported General Del Kemper's Artillery attack on the gun-boats *Paunee* and *Marblehead* in Ediston Inlet, Christmas, 1863. They supported another attack on the *Paunee* in Stone River several weeks later. On February 9th, the Cadet Company suffered casualties in a skirmish with Union Forces on John's Island.

The company's first service with the Army of Northern Virginia was pursuit of Sheridan during his last raid into the Shenandoah Valley. On June 11, 1864, the Confederates met the Union general at Louisa Court House and inflicted heavy losses. The following day, the Battle of Trevilians was fought fiercely and the part of the line held by the cadets yielded the greatest number of enemy dead. The cadets suffered seven wounded. The Sixth Regiment also fought at Lee's Mill, Gravel Run and Burgess' Mill, the last one being the last fight of "The Cadet Company in Virginia."

Upon its return to South Carolina, the company was involved in many skirmishes and the Battle of Bentonville. The Cadet Company then marched to the trans-Mississippi part of the Confederacy and disbanded, a unit which had held a unique place in the history of the Confederacy.

The last class to matriculate in the South Carolina Military numbered one hundred fourteen boys, ranging in age from fifteen to eighteen. Captain J. P. Thomas received them December 14, 1864, at the Arsenal Academy in Columbia and along with their studies guarded seven hundred Federal officer prisoners of war. Some of this final class had been in the Confederate Army and one of them, A. F. O'Brien, had lost his right arm in battle.

On February 16, 1865, the cadets were guarding the highway bridge across the Congaree River and were the targets of the Federal sharpshooters on the opposite side; the boys withdrew setting the bridge afire. With Sherman pressing down, Columbia was evacuated; the Arsenal Academy disappeared in the burning of the city by Sherman's army. The operations of the two schools ceased as of February 18, 1865.

Both battalions of the boys operated in military units for two months longer and then met up in Spartanburg. They finally marched to Greenville with the news of Lee's surrender.

Charleston fell on February 18, 1865, and although the Stars and Stripes flew over the Citadel, there were no cadets in residence as they were still in the field. Federal troops remained there seventeen years.

> We have seen that on January 1861–three months before the War began—it was a detachment of Citadel boys who fired the first hostile shot at the American flag when the steamer *Star of the West* attempted to relieve Fort Sumter. And four years of bloody strife, when the armies of the Confederacy were all dissolved and the war was over, the little band of Arsenal Cadets—the freshman class of the South Carolina Military Academy—was to fire the last hostile shot.
>
> On this first of May, after a weary march, not far from Williamston, near the spot where the Piedmont cotton mills now stand, the boys were resting—and some were asleep—when the bivouac was started by a sudden dash of the cavalry composing the advance guard of Stoneman's brigade. The spot where the Cadets were resting was around a curve in the road, and it is likely that the raiders were as much surprised as the Cadets when they rode thus

> unexpectedly upon a body of young men in uniform. They fired only a few shots and dashed on down the road, the affair lasting only a few minutes. Captain Thomas says, 'Some confusion incident to surprise ensued; but when the flag was displayed in the road, the command promptly rallied around it, and the fire was returned by the Cadets with effect.'[9]

And so, the boys who had fired first on the flag were in all probability the last to inflict a casualty upon the armed forces of the United States Government in the War of Secession.

C. The University of Alabama's Corps of Cadets

The University of Alabama founded as a civilian college in 1831 found it expedient to introduce a military system in the institution because the boys who had come from cotton plantation owners' families were spoiled, undisciplined and uninterested in learning.

Under the leadership of its first president, Dr. Landon Cabell Garland and with the final support of the Alabama legislature, the university became a military institution in 1860, three months before South Carolina seceded from the Union on the eve of the Civil War.

The cadets were trained by a West Pointer, First Lieutenant Caleb Huse, U.S. Army. Under his leadership, the Alabama Corps of Cadets emerged as a well-disciplined group of youngsters who were later to cover themselves with glory in the war.

In June of 1861, due to desertions because the cadets went off to join the regulars, Garland began admitting fourteen year olds. However, in that same month the cadets had trained nineteen Alabama companies. As with the case at The Citadel, the "deserters" formed their own groups in the Confederate Army, including Captain Charles P. Storr's Cadet Troop which fought throughout the war and Alabama cadets were the escort cavalry company of Captain Bascom T. Shockley. The cadets were again asked by the governor to train recruits and 12,000 of them were organized into thirty regiments of infantry and cavalry by the cadets.

The cadets saw action at the Battle of Chehaw in July, 1864, where two of their comrades were wounded and as a result of this action, the Alabama Corps of Cadets was formally accepted into the Confederate Army at Selma. They were used to guard railroads and bridges and then returned to Tuscaloosa in the fall of 1864 to resume their education.

The cadets were called "Katydids" because some veterans thought they looked like the insect when decked out in their dress uniforms. Because the graduates of the University of Alabama had gone into the Confederate Army, the Union felt that the university was a military training school which should be destroyed.

As the Union forces approached Tuscaloosa, the cadets were awakened by the long roll on the drum, and the cadets sprang from their beds and followed Garland and Colonel James Murfee, the commandant towards the oncoming enemy.

The two six pounders which made up the cadet battery (and had been left in the care of some army artillerymen home on leave) were seized by the Federals before the cadets could reach them.

The cadets fired towards the troops of General James T. Croxton at the Northport bridge and the Federal forces retreated, but Garland realized he was outnumbered and ordered the cadets to return to the campus.

Garland then ordered the cadets to prepare to march and they supplied themselves with food and ammunition and marched out of Tuscaloosa. Before their departure, the cadets destroyed all remaining ammunition.

The next morning, Croxton ordered the University of Alabama completely destroyed except for the president's home, the observatory and a few other buildings.

III. Music Boys, 1861-1916

When the Civil War burst upon the American scene, the romanticization of the military role of youth became permanently enshrined as a part of the glory of America's military endeavors. Prior to that time, there had been little written about the adventures of children in the armed forces. The Civil War left us with a cornucopia of letters, diaries, reminiscences, memoirs, pictures, and paintings. Most of those recordings are of boys who served in the volunteer units.

Not only were the boys' duties ill-defined after the start of the war, but enlistment procedures became equally confused. Despite an August 26, 1861 order from the Adjutant General's office, which the state volunteer units largely ignored, many boys entered without parental consent. On July 4, 1864, a new order was issued:

> The Act of July 4, 1864, Sec. 5 and the Act of March 3, 1864, Sec. 18 make it an offense to enlist any minor under the age of 16 years. It is recommended that this act be modified so far as to authorize a limited number, say 100 boys, but not under twelve years as musicians provided the consent of parent or guardian is previously obtained."[10]

In fact, those who enlisted legally were in the minority. Most of the youngsters were, in a manner of speaking, adopted by the regiments. Most were paid from the private funds of the commanding officer. This helps explain their change in status from musicians only, to barbers and orderlies as well.

Army musicians, called "Ponies" by the older men, fell into two classifications. Those who served with infantry and heavy artillery units included the drummers and fifers. Since drum beats were the dominant form of communication while in the camp or when the troops were on the march, the drummers and fifers were known as the "tongue of the camp". They were responsible for all the orders of the day including "reveille", "breakfast and dinner calls", "roll call", "quinine call" (aptly named for the medicine which seems to have been used as a cure-all) and finally "tattoo". Until 1862, the drummers were awakened by and responsible to the Principal Musician, but the band units were eliminated in that year due to the demand for fighting personnel caused by the war. After that time, they were apparently under the direction of the unit commander.

If a boy were the drummer for a company, his typical day would probably follow this pattern. After reveille at dawn, he would beat "breakfast call" followed by sick or quinine call. At about nine o'clock, he would fall in for "guard mount" and mark time for the troops as they marched or drilled. If the commanding officer wished to increase pace, he would have the drummer beat in double quick time. If he wanted a turn, the command for wheeling would be played. "Dinner call" followed at noon after which the drummer would have about five hours to practice or do duty as an orderly. Another dinner call was played at five p.m. followed by an eight p.m. roll call. The drummer would end his day by walking down the line of tents and gently beating tattoo.

Taps was composed at the Berkeley Plantation in Virginia by General Daniel Butterfield when he was stationed there in 1862 with McClellan's Army of the Potomac. He called his bugler and suggested he blow a refrain suitable for military funerals. Butterfield felt that music could replace the three volleys fired at military funerals and thus the Confederates would not know when a burial was taking place.

It is told that once the Confederates heard the refrain from their encampment on the opposite side of the James River, they repeated it because they liked the melodious yet sad sound of the music.

The second class of "ponies" were those assigned to cavalry and light artillery units. These were the buglers or the "tongue of the horsemen". Their duties greatly resembled those of the drummers with some exceptions. Normally, the day began with reveille followed by "assembly or roll call", then "breakfast, surgeon's and drill call" rounded out the morning. After "dinner call" at noon came "drill" at four, "recall" at five, "guard mounting" at five-thirty, "dress parade" at six-thirty, "tattoo" at nine and finally "lights out" at nine-thirty. Calls that differed from the drummer's included "boots and saddles" the signal for mounted drills or formation. "Stable call" and "water call" ordered the men to care for the horses. "The General" meant it was time to break camp and, of course, there was "trot", "gallop" and "charge".

Because of the importance of hearing the bugles in battle, buglers were most often older than drummers. They simply had more lung power even though some were very small. Because they were older, buglers would more likely take the place on the firing line which had been vacated by a fallen soldier.

Not only did the war expose the musicians to the dangers of battle to a greater extent than ever before, but it also made them witnesses to its tragedy. One of the new duties thrust upon the young boys was the harrowing role of medical assistant. With white handkerchiefs tied around their arms to signify their non-combatant status, they scurried around makeshift hospitals honing the surgeons' instruments, acting as anesthetists, and removing amputated limbs and dead bodies for burial. George T. Ulmer, a sixteen year old drummer boy from Maine told of his role as an anesthetist:

> It was a horrible task at first. My duty was to hold the sponge or "cone" of ether to the face of the soldier who was to be operated on and to stand there and see the surgeons cut and saw legs and arms as if they were cutting swine or sheep, was an ordeal I never wish to go through again. At intervals, when the pile became large, I was obliged to take a load of legs and arms and place them in a trench nearby for burial.[11]

Later, Ulmer would be forced to use his drumsticks to apply a tourniquet to the arms of another boy whose hands had been blown off. Unfortunately, the boy died as Ulmer read to him from the Bible. The passage was "suffer the little children to come unto Me."

C. W. Bardeen, fifer in Company D, First Massachussetts Infantry, held the parts of the anatomy that were to be removed:

> Theoretically it would be a difficult thing for us to hold a man's leg while it was being sawn off. Practically I did it here without shrinking much more easily than I could have looked on without holding the leg.[12]

The tremendous variety of uses that the units found for their musicians was quite amazing. Indeed, as some of the following stories illustrate, drumming and bugling often became a secondary occupation. Again, this utilization of the boys as sort of jacks-of-all-trades was primarily due to their unofficial status, the demands of war and the youngsters' sometimes irrepresible urge for adventure.

John Lincoln Clem (he had changed his middle name from Joseph to Lincoln at the start of the war) also known as "The Drummer Boy of Shiloh" or "The Drummer Boy of Shiloh and Chickamauga", probably stands out as the most famous "pony" of the Civil War. After running away from home at the age of nine, he tried to join the Army but was refused forthwith. A second attempt with the Third Ohio Volunteer Regiment was also a failure. He was finally accepted by the 22nd Michigan as an unofficial drummer boy for $13.00 per month. He appeared on no regimental muster rolls.

If excitement was what Johnny was looking for, he soon found it at the Battle of Pittsburg Landing near Shiloh Meeting. As the Union forces were being routed, Johnny's drum was smashed by a canonball. Still, he stood his ground and was soon joined by General Grant who screamed, "Johnny Shiloh won't run. Don't let a boy and his general stand here and fight alone." Indeed, Pittsburg Landing was the last position left to the Union. If the Confederates had taken it, escape would have been cut off, but Pittsburg

Landing held and when reinforcements arrived the next day, the Northerners captured Shiloh. Johnny Clem's stand was rewarded with a regular enlistment as a drummer boy in the United States Army.

After the bloody Battle of Shiloh, Clem marched into a rather fiercely fought engagement, Chickamauga. At first, he functioned as a marker. His job was to carry the guidon, a small streamer, behind which the lines were to form. In the midst of battle, however, he picked up a shortened musket. When a Confederate colonel charged on him and demanded his surrender, Clem swung the musket and knocked the colonel off his horse, reportedly killing him. Fortunately, the colonel was not killed and after the war he became a prominent Texas attorney. Later, when Clem was stationed at Fort Brown, they became friends. Because of the fictional reports of the colonel's death, Clem became known as Johnny Chickamauga.

Following this episode, the adjutant and aide-de-camp to the commander of Battery M, First Ohio Light Artillery, Eben P. Sturges, wrote a vivid account of Clem to his family:

> There is a little boy here in Chattanooga who reminds me somewhat of Howie as he was when I left home to go soldiering. His name is Johnny Clem, who was a drummer boy at Chickamauga and he shot a rebel colonel for which General Rosecrans promoted him. . . . When I'm downtown someday, I'll buy his picture and send it home. He rides around on horseback with a great pistol hung out his side after the fashion of a mounted orderly and considering how much is made of him, he doesn't seem to put on many airs.[13]

Clem went on to see more action. After making sergeant at the age of twelve, he fought at Perryville, Stone River, Resaca, Kenesaw Mountain, Atlanta and Nashville. He finished the war as a messenger for Grant who, when President, nominated him for West Point. When Clem was refused admission because of his deficient education, Grant commissioned him a lieutenant in the U.S. Army. He was the last veteran of the Civil War to retire from active service. Major General John Lincoln Clem retired in 1915.

If Clem was the most famous of these all around child musicians, Robert Henry Hendershot best exemplified their rambunctious spirit. He was twelve when the war started and he persuaded the captain of the troops stationed in his home town of Jackson, Michigan, to allow him to play the drum rolls for the recruits. He became so immersed in his temporary duty, that he learned the arms manual, the facings, the various troop alignments and all the duties of the soldier. All this despite the fact that Captain C. V. DeLand had refused to take him on as the permanent drummer boy because he was too small.

Refusing to accept defeat, Hendershot hid in a tool box near the engine of the train which was taking the Jackson troops to Indiana. He was finally discovered in Michigan City, Indiana, given a rigorous spanking by DeLand and a ticket back to Jackson and placed in the care of the baggage master. Hendershot responded by running out of the back door when the master was unloading at the front. After hiding in a lumber yard, he managed to get on a train and follow the regiment (which was later to become part of the Ninth Michigan Infantry), to Indianapolis. A Lieutenant Purdy discovered him in a persimmon tree gathering fruit for the men. Needless to say, DeLand was furious and told Hendershot to leave immediately. Hendershot promptly asked Captain O. C. Rounds of Company B to sign him on as a drummer. Hendershot had succeeded at last.

One of Hendershot's first acts was to take his newly supplied Colt revolver with him on an errand outside the camp and use it to turn a pig into pork. The farmer, understandably disturbed, protested and Hendershot received a week in the guardhouse. He was released after twenty-four hours.

This set the tone of what would end up to be the most colorful career of any boy in the war. Once again, Hendershot demonstrated the flexible positions of the youngsters.

Before it was over, he would not only serve as a musician, but as a spy, a thief, a rifleman, a forager, a sailor and an arsonist. He would survive fierce fighting, dank conditions in a Confederate prison and a bout with thyphoid fever. Many of these episodes were due to his own boisterous refusal to do anything except that which pleased him at the spur of the moment, but some came as a result of bravery.

A good example of Hendershot's bravery was exhibited very early on the Sunday morning of July 13, 1862. About eight hundred Yankees, a group consisting of six companies of the Ninth Michigan Volunteers, a squadron of the Fourth Kentucky Cavalry, the Third Minnesota Volunteers and Hewitt's First Kentucky Battery, were stationed in and around Murfreesboro, Tennessee. Colonel Lester, the commanding officer of the post, had made the unfortunate decision to separate the troops into two detachments. The Confederates, sensing a weakness in the Murfreesboro defenses, attacked Hendershot's regiment just before dawn. Hendershot, who had been a victim of a case of insomnia, saw the Confederates galloping towards the Union troops. He frantically beat a roll on his drum to awaken his comrades, but the Ninth Michigan was immediately stripped of its position and scattered. Now they would have to fight in small squads, thus precluding any opportunity to mount a counterattack of any force.

Hendershot saw the obvious danger and put down his drum to take up a musket. Although the piece was so heavy he could barely raise it to his shoulder, he kept loading and firing from four to eleven a.m., seven hours of non-stop shooting. Despite the Union efforts, however, the Confederates poured into the town square and surrounded the courthouse where the Northerners were holed up.

Still, the fighting raged on and Hendershot kept firing. It was then that he spied a Confederate colonel on the sidewalk in front of the building. The colonel, who refused to heed warnings to get out of the line of fire, fell dead with Hendershot's bullet in full view of the citizens of the southern town, a fact that would come into play later.

Eventually the Confederates took over the bottom story and set the courthouse ablaze. The Yankees had no choice but to surrender. Hendershot played upon the sympathies of Confederate General Forrest by asking to ride in a wagon rather than walk because of a case of diarrhea. He was given a mule team to drive and when he realized it was filled with sick Rebels he drove it at high speeds over the roughest places he could find before he ran the wagon off a bridge and into a stream, thus exposing the already sick men to a chill and the danger of drowning. Because he injured his leg, Hendershot was able to plead innocence and escaped being shot. Hendershot managed to escape in a rainstorm later than night and headed for Murfreesboro in search of his regiment. He was recognized by the citizens immediately, however, and forced to flee to Nashville where he awaited the Ninth Michigan.

But Hendershot was foolhardy as well and it was this foolhardiness which brought him fame. After reenlisting in the Army following a brief period as a civilian, Hendershot found himself in the Army of the Potomac, then under the command of General A. E. Burnside, marching toward the town of Fredricksburg in order to cut Lee off from an easy retreat to Richmond. The Federals ran into a stiff resistance, however, when they tried to place a pontoon bridge across the Rappahannock River several miles to the northeast of the town. Heavy sniper fire prevented the Federal forces from placing the pontoons across the river.

It was then that a call went out for volunteers to row the pontoons across the river and lodge them from the opposite bank. Hendershot ignored orders for the band and drum corps to remain in camp and wandered off toward the river. He helped push the first boat from shore, but slipped and fell into the water and was forced to hold on to the side of the boat until it reached the opposite shore.

When the bridge was finally completed, Hendershot charged up onto the shore and began burning and looting homes. His first foray yielded him a clock, two blankets and several other small items, all of which he placed in a boat and took back to camp. There, he took a gun and a cartridge box and recrossed the river. Once across, he ran from house to house, torching each one and plundering its contents until he spotted a man ready to shoot him. Hendershot managed to outwit his would-be killer, took him prisoner, marched him to the river, back to camp and wound up receiving praise from Burnside on a job well done. Immediately after Burnside ordered him to remain in camp, Hendershot again disobeyed, went back across the river, and charged into enemy fire with several regiments. He was soon wounded by a minnie ball, which broke his leg, and taken to Burnside's headquarters where he remained about two months.

The end result of Hendershot's daring was fame. He was billed as "The Drummer Boy of the Rappahannock", and Horace Greeley, then editor of the New York Tribune, wrote to Burnside asking him to send the boy to New York so that his newspaper could present Hendershot with the finest drum available. Hendershot stopped off in Washington on the way and met President Lincoln (who told him he looked small for a drummer boy), Secretary of War Stanton and Gideon Welles, Secretary of the Navy. Then it was on to Providence, Rhode Island and General Burnside's home to complete his recovery from the minnie ball. (Again, Burnside's personal attention underscores the attitude of an adopted son that most officers and men held with regards to the boys.)

When he finally arrived in New York, he received the promised drum from the Tribune Association. It was made by William C. Pond & Co. of New York, probably the most famous maker of military instruments at that time. Indeed, the drum was quite ornate:

> The shell of this drum is of pure silver, the hoops are of solid rosewood, both the batter and the snare heads are made of transparent calfskin so clear one can read through them, the braces are of a new and unique pattern, with a German silver crest on each cone; the snare fastener is of German silver.[14]

While still in New York, Phineas T. Barnum, the famous P. T. Barnum, who never let an opportunity go by, hired Hendershot to play several engagements. It was at one of these that the venerable General Winfield Scott met Hendershot and praised his bravery as well as his playing. Hendershot's New York adventure ended through the courtesy of a captain of an ocean steamer who invited the boy to go on a voyage to Liverpool, England. Hendershot stayed abroad for nearly a month.

Upon his arrival back in New York, Hendershot signed to play at Barnum's museum for eight weeks. After that engagement, he returned to Washington to visit the regiments of the Army of the Potomac which were stationed in the area. Lincoln introduced him to both Houses of Congress and Hendershot played the long roll for his audience. Things became quieter for Hendershot in Washington and eventually he determined that it was time to go back into the military for some excitement.

This time, Hendershot chose the U.S. Navy. He was assigned to the steamer *U.S.S. Fort Jackson* stationed near Fort Fisher. Soon after he came aboard, volunteers were sought for a secret mission to destroy some inland salt works. Characteristically, Robert Hendershot was one of the first to offer his services. Everything moved according to plan. The small boats used for the operation had no problems, and the demolition was carried out smoothly. Typically, Hendershot decided he was in the midst of a good opportunity for scavenging souvenirs and he was left behind while searching. After realizing his predicament and seeing the boats move further and further out to sea, he decided to swim to an island. Fortunately for our hero, he was rescued by a group of marines who were ordered by the captain of the ship to rescue him.

Since Hendershot did not care much for the Navy and, understandably, the Navy didn't care much for him, he was discharged after only six months. He lived in Washington for about six months and then used his influence with Lincoln to maneuver himself into a job as news agent aboard the steamer *City Point.* It was on one of his trips to the lines that Hendershot volunteered to spy for Grant. Reportedly, the General said if Hendershot would ". . . dare go into rebel lines, you are the boy I want."

Before Hendershot got his chance to spy, however, he was captured. Part of his duty as a news agent was to deliver packages and boxes to the troops. One such box was addressed to a soldier at the front lines of Petersburg, Virginia. Hendershot delivered it, but decided to spend the night there as well. At four a.m., the Confederates attacked and Hendershot was taken prisoner. He was first taken to Petersburg, then to Castle Thunder and finally to the infamous Libby prison, second only to Andersonville in its reputation for cruelty. After about twenty days at Libby, Hendershot was quite ragged and dirty. He asked permission to bathe in the James River which, because he had played the drum for some of the guards, was granted. Once in the river, he swam until the following day when he reached the Union lines and was placed in the guardhouse on suspicion of spying.

The misunderstanding was settled when Grant came to see the boy who proceeded to tell the general everything he heard and saw while in the hands of the Confederates. This resulted in two ventures into the southern capital of Richmond for Hendershot; one posing as a dirty boot black. Grant was so impressed with him, that he recommended him for an appointment to West Point, something Generals Burnside and Spinner had already done.

While awaiting his appointment, Hendershot went back to his old job on the *City Point* for a brief period before returning to the field as a medical assistant for the Battles of Dinwiddie Courthouse, Five Forks and Welden Rail Road. After the war, he returned to the *City Point,* but the appointment to the Military Academy was not to be. He was rejected because of the wound in his leg he had received at Fredricksburg and even his appeal to President Johnson was to no avail. His friend, Abraham Lincoln, would probably have seen to his admission, but Johnson had problems of his own with Congress.

Before he had enlisted in the Navy, Hendershot had attended Eastman Business College in Poughkeepsie, New York. He returned after his appeal to Johnson was rejected and then went on to St. Lawrence University and a successful career with the Post Office. He never stopped playing his drum, however, and eventually decided to entertain full time with his son who played the fife.

Aside from Johnny Clem and Robert Hendershot, the best known boy hero of the Civil War was probably Orion P. Howe of the 55th Illinois Regiment. His father, a fifer and his ten year old brother Lyston, a drummer, had both gone off to war and left Orion in charge of his uncle's farm. It wasn't long before Orion had left his life on the farm and set out on a six-week journey from Waukegan, Illinois to Memphis, Tennessee, where his father and brother were stationed. There, he joined his brother, each drumming for their respective companies, in the 55th Illinois, a regiment that became a part of Grant's army that fought in the Vicksburg Campaign.

Once the 55th reached Vicksburg, the regimental commander, Colonel Oscar Malmborg, ordered the musicians, all of whom were supposed to be in the rear, to carry fresh cartridges up to the front. It was thought they would be able to negotiate the rough ground and the paths which were strewn with fallen trees. Because Orion was already at the front when the order was given, he did not hear of it until sometime later when he was giving water to the wounded. Rather than take new boxes of cartridges to the front, Orion thought it would be wiser to collect the unused cartridges from the dead and wounded in the area. When he reached the ordnance wagon with his load, he decided to set out again. As the regimental historian states:

> Again he sped down across the ravine and up the steep opposite slope. We would see him nearly the whole way as he ran through what seemed like a hailstorm of canister and musket balls, so thickly did these fall about him, each throwing up the little

> puff of dust where it struck the hillside. Suddenly he dropped, and hearts sank thinking his brief career ended; but he had only tripped over some obstacle. Often he stumbled, sometimes he fell prostrate but was quickly up again, and the Fifty-fifth saw him no more for several months. As the boy sped away the last time the Colonel shouted to him as he alleges 'Bring calibre fifty-four![15]

It later turned out that "calibre fifty-four" was inaccurate because the rifles of the regiment were all calibre fifty-eight but the romanticizing of the event made the fifty-four story more appropriate to the occasion.

The regiment would not see him for months because he was wounded in the leg. He later became an orderly at the headquarters of General Giles A. Smith after being promoted to corporal on his fifteenth birthday. He was wounded again on May 28, 1864, at Dallas. This time, he was hit twice in the right arm and once in the breast. He received a citation for "his usefulness at the Battle of Resaca".

While in the hospital, Orion was notified that he had been recommended for the Naval Academy (it had a lower entrance age than West Point) but because of his lack of education, he had to be given a year's extension before taking the entrance examination, and once he did become a cadet, he was forced to leave after two years for failing the required courses. He then drifted from occupation to occupation. He became a merchant seaman, a cowboy, an Indian fighter, and lastly a dentist. Finally, in 1896, the decision was made to award Orion P. Howe, the Congressional Medal of Honor.

One facet of Howe's story serves to shed light on the treatment the boys of the Civil War received. It has already been demonstrated that the officers often made themselves responsible for the youngsters, but the historian of the Fifty-fifth Illinois maintains that:

> The little Howes, our infant drummers, drummed well, proved hardy, never seemed homesick, were

> treated as pets and passed through march after march, untouched by disease, unscathed by bullet and shell.[16]

Howe was not the only boy to win the Medal of Honor. In fact, several other youngsters proved themselves worthy of the nation's highest honor. The youngest of these was twelve year old Private Willie Johnston, Musician, Company D, 3rd Vermont Infantry who enlisted to see his father who had been wounded at Lee's Mill, Virginia. He ended up in the Army of the Potomac fighting in the Peninsular Campaign under General George B. McClellan.

Little Willie experienced harrowing all night marches, daylong fighting, frontal assaults, flank attacks and unusually fierce artillery fire in heavy, dense fog and muddy terrain but through it all, he managed to keep his drum safe and sound, the only drummer to do so. All others had discarded theirs because of the weight the drums added and the terribly difficult conditions. After the campaign, when the troops were camped at Hansen's Landing, there was a parade on Independence Day. Willie Johnston was the only drummer chosen to beat out the steps for the thousands of soldiers who paraded before General McClellan. He later received the Medal of Honor for "Gallantry in the Seven Days' Fight and Peninsular Campaign, May-June, 1862".

Another Medal of Honor winner, William H. Horsfall, was one of many faced with an important decision at the start of war because he lived in Kentucky, a border state. Soon after hostilities broke out, Billy made his decision and ran away from his home in Newport, just across the Ohio River from Cincinnati, in search of the First Kentucky Infantry. He crossed the river, but the regiment, which had just been accepted by Lincoln and trained and equipped at the expense of Ohio, had already gone on to Virginia. Ohio recruits gave Horsfall rations and money, then sent him up the river on a transport. When he reached the First Kentucky, he was accepted by Company G to replace a drummer who had fallen ill.

Because he was only four feet, three inches tall, Private

Horsfall was nearly lost in his uniform. His trousers had to be rolled up, his jacket flowed over his tightened belt and because he could find no shoes to fit his feet, he went barefoot while in the Army. Even his drum was too large. He was constantly stumbling over it and his knees developed huge calluses from the beating they took. This was the boy who would go on to be a hero.

Horsfall underwent his baptism of fire at Shiloh, but it was his performance at Corinth, Mississippi that earned him the medal. During the battle, Private Horsfall put away his drum and, because he had learned to be a marksman back home in Kentucky, picked up a gun. While on the firing line, Horsfall witnessed his captain, James Williamson, fall with a wound in the hip. Lieutenant Louis Hocke, apparently forgetting Horsefall's size, told Billy to move forward and rescue the captain. Despite the hail of bullets, he managed to reach the captain, but because of the disparity in sizes, he had to drag Captain Williamson short distances and then rest at intervals. After several minutes, he reached the Union stretcher bearers and the captain was saved. When he was acclaimed as a hero, he claimed that he "...was only obeying the lieutenant's orders". He was discharged in 1864 at the age of sixteen, but it was thirty-one years before he received his Medal of Honor.

Another boy, John Christopher Julius Langbein, a German immigrant, also won the Medal of Honor by rescuing his commanding officer. Indeed, Langbein's story again emphasizes the close, almost father-son, relationship that grew between the boys and their commanders.

At the start of the war, when states were forming volunteer regiments, Hawkin's Zouaves, officially known as the 9th New York Infantry, was also taking shape at Castle Garden, New York. Julius Langbein was a frequent visitor to the parade ground because he was attracted to the distinctive uniforms. They featured a tassled scarlet fez, a short blue jacket and a shirt embroidered in black. A red silk sash was tied around the waist and loose, baggy trousers were tucked into white garters. It was on one of these visits that

Langbein met Lieutenant Thomas Bartholomew of Company B who eventually persuaded Langbein's widowed mother to consent to her son's enlistment by promising that he would see to it that Julius would be carried on long marches or ride in the supply wagon and that he would eat in the officer's mess.

In the swamps of Camden, North Carolina, Bartholomew would have reason to rejoice over his bargain for it was there that Julius, called "Jennie" because his almost feminine German features, led him to the role of Jennie in the regimental plays, set out under heavy fire and carried Bartholomew back to the doctor only to have the surgeon give the lieutenant up for dead and turn his attention to loading the less seriously wounded on to an army wagon. (This practice, known as triage, is still used today. If a man is not seriously wounded, or if there is little chance of saving him, the attending physician moves on to more urgent cases in an effort to maximize survivors.) Julius, however, would not let his leader die. Bartholomew states that Julius:

> . . . came quietly to my bedside and whispered, 'Keep quiet, Lieutenant, you shall not be left behind. I have arranged it all.' And he hurriedly left the room. I did keep quiet, for I trusted him fully. I heard a wagon stop at the door. Some comrades carried out the other wounded and I was left alone. . . . Jennie soon came, and with him, two other drummers who quietly but quickly took me from the bed. Before I could think how it was done, I was placed in the rear end of the wagon . . . I was actually squeezed in just as the wagon started. I have never asked Jennie how he concocted and carried out his scheme, but I know that he alone saved my life and I can never repay him.[17]

Later, Langbein himself would barely escape death. At the Battle of Antietam, his horse was shot out from under him, at Fredricksburg, his drum was riddled by bullets, and at the Battle of Suffolk, the tassel of his fez was shot away.

As regimental commander Colonel Rush C. Hawkins wrote in a personal letter to Secretary of War Stanton:

> I consider this young man in the light of a natural soldier, full of the proper spirit, and a natural true soldierly pride and above all truthful and honest and faithful in the discharge of his duty. I am sure he will make a good soldier.[18]

General Burnside offered to take Langbein to Washington to meet with Lincoln regarding a West Point berth but the President was killed before it could be arranged. Langbein went on to become a lawyer, and received his medal in 1894.

Another boy who won the medal for rescuing his comrades under fire later became famous for another reason. Julian A. Scott spent the early part of the war in Washington as a musician in Company E of the Third Vermont Infantry. In the spring of 1862, however, the regiment was called away from its assignment of guarding the Chain Bridge connecting Washington, D.C. and Virginia. He was attached to the Army of the Potomac so it could take part in the Peninsular Campaign. Scott carried a sketchbook along with his drum and began refining an already apparent artistic talent by sketching other soldiers, horses, weapons and their surroundings.

At one point in the offensive, during the Battle of Lee's Mill, the Union forces became bogged down in an area filled with small ponds resulting from the damming of Warwick Creek. In order to extricate themselves, Companies D, E, F and K of the 3rd Vermont charged out of the surrounding woods and ran to the creekside. Here they were forced to unclasp their ammunition belts, hold both their cartridges and their guns in the air and wade across the waist deep creek while being fired upon by Confederate snipers. Once they reached the opposite bank, they managed to rout the resistance.

Unfortunately, the captain ordered an end to the pursuit because he feared an overextension of troops and preferred to wait for reinforcements. They didn't arrive in time, so the Southerners took the opportunity of the cease fire to regroup and counterattack. It was then that the Yankees discovered that much of their ammunition had become waterlogged in their trek across the stream. Even when the remaining dry ammunition had been doled out, the Unionists could not move because they were hemmed in on three sides, had the water to their backs, half their force on the other side and were being showered with gunfire.

Julian Scott was one of those on the other side. As the beleaguered captain frantically sent messenger after messenger across the water to ask the colonel for reinforcements so he could engineer an escape, Scott sprang into action. He dropped his drum and dashed across the stream to rescue the wounded who were trapped in the gunfire. The first soldier was too heavy for him to carry so he dragged the man to, then across the river. The second was able to lean against the young Scott and wade. Scott went back and forth across the river, often stepping on the bodies of dead men who had been submerged in the muddy water. The smoke was so thick that Scott could not even identify the men he was rescuing, but he continued to carry men on his shoulders like sacks of flour. When the reinforcements had finally arrived and the escape completed, Scott had rescued nine men, most of whom would certainly have died, and delivered them to the doctors.

In 1863, during his service as an orderly to General William Smith, Scott was wounded. While recuperating in a New York hospital, he filled the walls with chalk and charcoal murals. Word of Julian's ability spread and Mr. Henry E. Clark, a lawyer, visited Scott and came away impressed by his talent. He offered to sponsor formal art studies for Scott and asked the surgeons to release him from the hospital. In April of 1863, Scott was mustered out of the army. He was seventeen.

Julian Scott went on to tour battle sites with the New York representatives of the United States Sanitary Commission, the forerunner of the American Red Cross, and filled his sketches with the drama of what he witnessed.

After being awarded the Medal of Honor for his action at Lee's Mill in 1862 he studied under Emmanuel Leutze, painter of "Washington Crossing the Delaware," who sent him to Berlin to continue with his studies. Upon his return, he opened a studio in New York and his reputation grew. He now stands as one of America's greatest military artists. Some of his paintings include "The Rear Guard at White Oak Swamp," "Cavalry Charges at the Toll Gate Near Ashkip Gap, Virginia," "Hancock at the Battle of Williamsburg," and "The American Cornfield," all of which Scott had fought in while still a soldier.

Some of his paintings depict the role he knew best, that of the young musicians. These included "The Rescue of the Color Bearer," "The Drummer" and "The Bugler." In the "Death of General Sedgwick" Scott placed grieving drummer and stretcher boys in the background.

Scott's most famous painting is probably his rendition of the charge of the Vermont Brigade at the Battle of Cedar Creek in the Shenandoah Valley which hangs in the Vermont State House. So impressed were the legislators, that they paid Scott $4,000 more than the original commission of $5,000. Scott became one of the few men who could change tragedy into beauty.

Two youngsters won the nation's highest decoration for bravery during incidents involving their regimental colors. These colors, six and one-half by six feet and mounted on a ten-foot staff, held military as well as emotional significance for the Union troops. The flags were used as signals for the troops to move up when their ranks had broken. Commanding officers would shout the order: "Men, follow your colors" as an order to charge forward against the enemy. If troops became panic stricken, disorganized, or threatened to run, the commander would stand by the flag, which served as a beacon, and order the soldiers to "Form on the colors." For this reason, the flags were always held aloft, and, if the bearer was killed or wounded, the flag was seized by one of the color guard. If he fell, any soldier or officer was obliged to seize the flag and keep marching forward:

> Each regiment and division had two color bearers guarded by seven soldiers, the color guard, selected for their devotion and coolness under fire. In battle formation the two color bearers, one holding the national, the other the regimental flag in front of the troops, were flanked by a guard to their left and right. The highest ranking commanding officer, usually a colonel on foot or mounted on horseback, took his place near them. The first line of soldiers formed six paces behind. Four of the color guard were just behind them, so they could go to the rescue of the imperiled bearer. A single guard was posted in front of the next line of soldiers.[19]

On an emotional level, nearly all soldiers were devoted to their colors. Whenever a new unit was formed, the men were told that there was no greater dishonor than the lowering of the flag and no disgrace worse than having it fall into the hands of the enemy. In view of these facts, it seems a small wonder that more than a tenth of the 1200 Civil War Medals of Honor were awarded to color bearers or soldiers who picked it up and advanced with it into battle.

The first of the two boys to win the medal was Benjamin Levy, a sixteen year old New York lad who followed his fourteen year old brother into the Army by enlisting in October, 1861, at Newport News, Virginia as a drummer. Later, he became an orderly to Brigadier General Joseph Mansfield and eventually served as a courier between Mansfield and Major General John Wool, Mansfield's superior at Fort Monroe. It was on such a mission that Levy saved the Army boat *Express,* himself and the sensitive dispatches regarding troop movements he carried, from certain capture by cutting a howser and releasing a boat being towed by the *Express.* If he hadn't cut the cable, the Confederate gunboat *Sea Bird* would have overrun the slower Union vessel.

This quick action by Levy was a precedent to his fast thinking and bravery at the Battle of Glendale in the White Oak Swamp. Before the battle, Levy's tentmate had fallen ill with a case of malaria and Benjamin decided to replace him. As the battle raged, all the color bearers except two had become casualties. Then, one of the remaining two was hit and Levy rushed forward and seized the colors from the wounded man only to witness the last of the color bearers receive a hit. Levy instantly dropped his gun, picked up the other standard and ran both colors back to the Union lines despite being wounded on the way back. He was found by General Philip Kearney as he emerged from the woods. Kearney carried him back to headquarters and promoted him to Color Sergeant on the spot.

Later, at the Battle of Malvern Hill, Levy was in the color guard. Because the regiment had been marching and fighting for such an extended period, their uniforms were covered with dust. They were so dirty in fact that the Union batteries mistook them for Confederates and opened fire. In desperation, Colonel Dyckman ordered Levy to march out into the middle of the battlefield and show the colors. Fortunately for the regiment, and especially for Levy, the firing stopped immediately. As he turned to return to the lines, however, the Confederates began firing. Bullets hit the flag staff, the peak of his cap and his tin cup. He instantly dropped to the ground, took the colors from the staff, rolled it up and tied it with strips torn from his handkerchief. Then, he turned himself into a barrel and rolled all the way back to his wildly cheering comrades.

Two months later, however, he would not be so lucky. He was wounded for the second time, at the Battle of Chantilly. When his enlistment expired in May of 1863 he was mustered out only to return before the year was out. This time, he enlisted in the "Mozart" regiment, the 40th New York Infantry, a group made up mostly of Germans. Soon afterwards, he was promoted to sergeant but serious wounds, the third of his brief service, suffered at the vicious Battle of the Wilderness ended his career as a soldier. He received his Medal of Honor in March of 1865.

Young Nathaniel Gwynne also won the medal because of an action in the defense of his colors. In fact, he was the only boy cavalry bugler to win the medal during the Civil War and yet, like many others, he was not really in the Army at the time he earned the award. After he ran away from his home in Urbana, Ohio, and traveled the nearly one hundred miles to Cincinnati, he found the 13th Ohio Volunteer Cavalry and begged the commanding officers of each company to accept him. He worked his way up the alphabet and was refused by each until First Lieutenant William Mark, commander of Company H, agreed to take him on providing that Gwynne learn to play all the calls. But when the men of his unit were sworn in to the service, Gwynne's name was not called. Still, he accompanied the 13th to Washington where they learned that they would fight as dismounted cavalry because of a lack of horses.

Nathaniel had seen some action at the Second Battle of Cold Harbor, but because he was not officially a member of the regiment and because he had not yet mastered the special calls on his trumpet, he played only those necessary for the troops in the camp. During the follow-up attack on the Petersburg Mine in Virginia, however, he decided to disobey orders to stay in camp and chose to advance toward the enemy. "No sir," he told his commanding officer, "I'm of too good stock to lumber in the rear." When the regiment's chief bugler sounded 'charge,' Gwynne ran across a ravine, up a hill and into the view of the enemy cannon. The battle turned against the Union forces and the regimental flag was captured. Gwynne turned his back on his retreating comrades and faced the pursuing enemy. He ran at the Confederate who held the captured colors, struck him in the jaw and clubbed him with his musket at the same time. Gwynne grabbed the banner from the fallen man and headed back for his own lines with every enemy gun aimed at him. So many bullets struck the arm that held the flag that it was almost shot away and Gwynne dropped the colors. When he picked them up with his good arm, he was shot in the leg so he had to crawl the rest of the way back to his own troops. When he reached the line at last, he lost consciousness.

Nathaniel Gwynne's arm was amputated after the battle

and his brief military career ended at the age of fifteen. He was finally mustered into the Army on January 3, 1865, and the order was made retroactive to May of 1864 when he first stepped into Company H. He received the Medal of Honor that same January day.

One boy won the medal, not by saving his own colors, but by capturing the enemy's flag. Harry Jeremiah Parks had run away from his family's farm in New York state to enlist and make use of his expertise at horsemanship. He joined under the name of Jeriamiah Parks and became a part of Troop A, 9th New York Cavalry under the command of General George A. Custer on the Rapidan River in Virginia. There, Parks acted as a scout, a raider and a fighter.

Eventually, the 9th New York moved north to join Sheridan at Winchester, Va., the northern opening of the Shenandoah Valley. When the Federals had succeeded in routing the enemy, Sheridan issued orders that all Union material that had been captured by the rebels was to be retaken. The 9th New York Cavalry set out after the Confederates, but Troop A, Parks included, became separated from the main force and soon Parks discovered that he had gone too far and ridden into a group of Confederate soldiers. Camouflaged by the darkness, Parks stumbled across the Confederate flag bearer and forced him to surrender at gunpoint. After he marched his prisoner back to the Union lines, he returned to the Confederate forces and duped three teamsters into believing he was an officer. They obeyed his order to follow him and drove themselves directly into the Federal lines. He had single handedly captured the color bearer and three wagons full of supplies in one night.

While many boys joined the Army to put distance between themselves and their parents or joined in spite of their elders' efforts to stop them, some youngsters enlisted with their parents' blessing and, in some cases, their parents signed up with them. Such was the case with Robinson E.B. Murphy, Musician, Company A, 10th Illinois Infantry. Murphy's father opposed his son's enlistment at first. Indeed, he had stopped Robinson from joining on two separate occasions, but he finally allowed his thirteen year old, four-foot six-inch son to enlist and he, at age fifty-one, did the same even though it meant giving up a law practice to enter the Army as a private.

Robinson served as a drummer and as an orderly to the colonel of the regiment at Vicksburg. Later, he was assigned to General Joseph A. Lightburn, brigade commander of the XVth Corps of the Union Army. After a month's recuperation from back injuries suffered in a train accident, he reported to Lightburn even though it meant being separated from his father.

Because of his duty as a messenger for Lightburn, he was sent to most of the units of the Army of the Tennessee at one time or another and had many opportunities to study and learn the maps that had been marked with troop movements and battle plans.

Murphy's experience at headquarters would come in handy at the Battle of Ezra Chapel near Atlanta. The fight was turning against the Northerners. Lightburn's division was caught in a devastating cross-fire and was unable to help the 127th Illinois, the elder Murphy's regiment, which was in imminent peril of being cut off from the rest of the army. If this happened, heavy casualties would be inflicted. Robinson realized the danger of the situation and begged Lightburn to help his father's unit. Because Lightburn was already involved in a critical situation, he sent him to General Logan for help.

When he reached Logan's group, he explained the urgency of the situation. Logan immediately sent for reinforcements and ordered Robinson to meet them. Not only did he meet the relief troops (Ohio regiments), he also brought them to the weakened points in the line and then led them in a charge. Even after his horse was killed, he continued to lead the charge yelling "Follow me!" and running ahead of the replacements. Thanks to Murphy's knowledge of the maps and his quick action, his father's regiment was saved. His citation read: "Being orderly to the brigade commander, he voluntarily led two regiments as reinforcements into the line of battle where he had his horse shot out from under him." Robinson Murphy, the fifteen year old who had led two regiments into battle, later became an orderly to Sherman's chief of staff, General Joseph Webster, during the March to the Sea.

One young Medal of Honor winner however not only demonstrated his bravery in one battle, but performed bravely throughout the most fiercely contested and bloody battles of the four year war. Fourteen year old John Cook, bugler for Battery B of the 4th U.S. Artillery (Cook was the only teenage artillery bugler to win the medal who belonged to a Federal, not a state regiment) joined up in June of 1861 and eventually became an orderly to Lieutenant James Stewart, the commander of one of the two gun sections. (Battery B was a mounted light artillery unit with 150 officers and enlisted men, six guns, twelve caissons and a limber for each. This type of six gun battery was divided into threes, each section having two guns each.) Cook's job was to ride along the line with Stewart and to transmit firing orders to distant gun emplacements. One member of the battery recalled the image of Cook on his horse:

> Johnnie rode a bob-tailed pony which we always hated to see in the line of battle because she made a center target for the enemy's shells. . . . 'Get that damn ghost out of sight!' the officer would yell sometimes, when the enemy would begin to reach for little John and his white pony with their shells.[20]

At the Battle of Antietam, however, the troops would be happy to see Bugler Cook. During the battle, he was acting as a courier to the battery commander, Captain Joseph Campbell, and assisting in the coordination between the sections of guns which had been set up: one on a pike, the other in a field. As the captain and Cook rode, the officer's horse was suddenly shot out from under him, leaving the captain badly wounded. Johnny, only five feet tall, lifted the captain and carried him all the way to the ambulance driver in the rear. Once there, Campbell told Cook to tell Lieutenant Stewart what had happened and to take over the coordination of the gun sections.

As Cook rode between emplacements, he discovered two unmanned guns and began to serve them. He acted as the sponger (by cleaning the vent with grease), the rammer (by pushing in the shell and the powder charge), the cannoneer (by priming the gun), and the gunner (by sighting for distance and trajectory and jerking the lanyard). While single handedly performing the functions of four men, Cook was spotted by Brigadier General John Gibbon who jumped off his horse and began serving the guns with Cook. The general and the bugler fired the cannons until the end of the battle. Lieutenant Stewart later testified that Cook's "...courage and conduct in that battle won the admiration of all who witnessed it."

Johnnie later demonstrated that same "courage and conduct" in many other conflicts such as Fredricksburg, Chancellorsville, the Wilderness and Spotsylvania Court House. He also fought at Gettysburg where, through a show of daring, he destroyed Union ammunition which was sure to be captured. Johnnie's last fight was the Battle of Bethesda Church. The regimental historian points a vivid picture of Johnnie as the battle began:

> It was at least his twentieth battle, and he was still less than seventeen years old. Literally, Johnnie had more battles than his years. His time was out, he had his honorable discharge in his pocket, and was only awaiting transportation to go home.
>
> But his bugle never sounded so loud and clear as it did when he followed the captain and blew 'Forward, trot!' and 'Forward, gallop!' as our horses stretched their necks out for that rebel battery on the pike.[21]

Despite the captain's superstition that a discharged man should not tempt fate and ride into battle, "...Johnnie had got that old scent of powder up his nose once more and nothing could stop him."

> So away he went, following the Old Man along the pike and blowing his bugle as lustily as ever, while

> the enemy's canister cut down the brush by the side of the road or screamed over our heads. And when we finally limbered our guns and made them 'talk', Johnnie was everywhere as usual, riding back and forth along the line of battle, as fresh and eager as if he were a tenderfoot rather than a veteran.[1]

Johnnie Cook betrayed the captain's superstition and lived to receive his Medal of Honor in 1894.

Many boys did not find glory or fame like those mentioned above, but met the tragic reality of war instead. Young boys, like George Ulmer (who had his uniform made and covered it with gold braid and ornaments so he looked more like a drum major than a drummer boy), ran with native bravado into the conflict but many returned with shattered bodies or with disillusioned hearts much older than their years. And, of course, some died. These boys lived up to General Sherman's epigram and proved that "War is hell."

Charley King was one such boy. He was a twelve year old drummer boy in the 49th Pennsylvania Infantry when he was wounded at Antietam. He died three days later. Samuel Sufshay, a Negro drummer boy, was killed on July 15, 1864. (Several negro drummer boys served in the war. Union troops marching through the South would adopt those they found, and some, like Alexander Johnson and Thomas Edward Platner, served with the famous Fifty-fourth Massachusetts Colored Infantry.) Clarence McKenzie of Company B, New York State Militia, was also twelve when he was killed by the accidental discharge of a gun that a friend had been using to practice a bayonet charge. The ball was forced into Clarence's back and he lived only two more hours.

> As the coffin was taken from the drummer's quarters, preceded by the balance of the drum corps and a fifer playing the slow and solemn tune of the dead march, the other companies of the regiment fell into line and followed it to the cars. . . many a man, who would not flinch on the field of battle, shed tears

> over the remains of poor Clarence. He was the smallest in the corps and liked by everyone who knew him. . . I understand this is the second boy his parents have lost within a short time. His drum and knapsack have been tastily hung with crepe and wreaths of flowers out of respect by his comrades.[23]

And then there is the story of a boy whose devotion to his father cost him his life. His father served with a battery which happened to be camped near the drummer boy's unit at Spotsylvania. Realizing that his father was not allowed a fire to boil coffee (because of the proximity of gunpowder) the boy would take coffee to his father along with some salt pork and hardtack. One evening, however,

> He was admonished not to remain on the hill for any time as our men expected the rebels to open on them at any moment; but the faithful boy had reached his father, and wanted to wait and bring his coffee bottle with him for future use. Contrary to his father's warning, he waited until the coffee was drank, and just as he was ready to leave, the rebels opened their batteries on that position, the first shell striking the brave boy and killing him on the spot.[24]

Disease also took quite a toll among the boys. Charles P. Dutchess, for example, was a drummer for the 25th New Jersey Volunteer Infantry until he was pressed into service as a hospital steward at Falmouth, Virginia, during the Battle of Fredricksburg. There he caught typhoid fever, a disease which had been running rampant in the ranks. The fever left him with holes in his hip and caused him to limp for the rest of his life, but despite his injuries, he eventually became a prominent doctor and surgeon. Private W. B. Smith, Company K, 14th Illinois Volunteer Infantry was wounded at fifteen, but it was the combination of the wound and his imprisonment at Millen, Blackshear and the infamous Andersonville prisons and their horrible conditions that left him in a wheelchair for the rest of his life.

Delevan Miller tells of one of his fellow drummer boys stationed with the Second New York Infantry who fell ill during the Bull Run Campaign. Although he struggled in the hospital for weeks;

> . . . when he realized that he must answer the last roll call, he wished the surgeon to send for his comrades of the drum corps. It was his wish that we should stand at parade rest in the aisle between the cots. From under his pillow he took a little Bible and opening it at the 23rd Psalm, handed it to Harry Marshall, our drum major, and motioned for him to read the beautiful words. Need I say that there were no dry eyes? And I think from that moment, life to most of the boys present had a more serious meaning.
>
> The next Sabbath afternoon, with muffled drums and slow measured tread, we escorted his remains to a little knoll 'neath a clump of pines near Arlington.[25]

Even for those boys who were not killed, wounded, captured or crippled by disease, life could still be hard. One drummer boy, William Bircher

> . . . had no shoes, so I tore up my shirt and wrapped it around my bleeding feet, they being so sore that I could not march without great pain.[25]

Bircher's Christmas in 1862 was:

> ". . . a gloomy one for us. We had our dinner, a bill of fare consisting of baked beans, coffee, hardtack and sow belly."[26]

While most of the boys served admirably, some became delinquents, and therefore burdens to their outfits. Some became incorrigible gamblers, undoubtedly through the influence of the older men. While some boys, like Robert Hendershot and George Ulmer, were taught to steal for the benefit of the unit, others became profiteers by selling provisions or items stolen from nearby farms, to the troops. Some even tempted the death penalty by deserting. Although Lincoln recognized that boys will be boys and suggested that the deserters be spanked and sent home (indeed, he actually saved several), some boys were still shot.

Several boys even ran businesses on the side. One, Doc Aubrey, became the regularly appointed agent for the sale of the New York Herald, the Baltimore American, the Washington Chronicle and the Philadelphia Inquirer. He was issued passes through the lines by order of General Patrick, the Provost Marshal General.

The last survivor of the Grand Army of the Republic was a drummer boy with the First Minnesota Heavy Artillery. His name was Albert Woolson and he died in 1956.

IV. The Boys Of The Confederacy 1861-1865

Some recognition must be given to the youngsters who fought in the Confederate Army, but not as much is known about the Confederate "cubs" because records about them are sparse. Due to the lack of education among Southern boys, few diaries were kept and few retrospectives were written, and the South had a more urgent need for "shooters than tooters." Many young Confederates were fighting on the front lines at a very early age and, as was true with most of the Confederate Army, conditions were usually very cruel. Fifteen year old quarter guard David E. Johnston explains how he got a new uniform after the First Battle of Manassas:

> I went out to help gather up the wounded and to get me a pair of trousers and shoes, both of which I had need of, and which I procured, selecting a dead Union soldier about my size. His shoes I could not wear, as they were too small, and I gave them back to a comrade; and I almost regretted having put on his trousers, for they were inhabited by the same sort of graybacks common to the Confederate and Union soldiers.[27]

There were very few musicians in the Confederate ranks,

but one, J. B. Thomas, a drummer boy, seized the musket of a fallen comrade at Gettysburg and shot the color bearer of one of the advancing Federal regiments at Missionary Ridge. Another drummer boy, William Nelson Boswell, entered the Confederate Army at age eleven to join his father's company in Pickett's unit of the Fifth Virginia Regiment. Jefferson Davis presented Boswell with a sword.

Charles Carter Hay joined an Alabama regiment in 1861 at age eleven and surrendered one month short of his fifteenth birthday in 1865. Sixteen year old Private Edwin Jemison of Georgia died at the Battle of Malvern Hill in Virginia. Matthew J. McDonald, known as "Mollie" was a fourteen year old cavalryman with Company I of the 1st Georgia Cavalry before he was captured in January of 1865 and held prisoner until June of that year. George S. Lamkin was only twelve when he suffered serious wounds at Shiloh and another twelve year old, John Bailey Tyler, is believed to be the youngest cavalryman of the war. He served in Troop D, 1st Maryland Confederate Cavalry and was later taken prisoner.

As the Union forces were converging on Atlanta, Georgia Governor Joseph E. Brown called into active service, the old men of the state up to age fifty-five and boys down to sixteen years old.

These youngsters were armed with flint-lock muskets, ordinary rifles and shotguns and ordered to the battlefront, where they took part in the defense of Atlanta.

The Confederate boys, like the rest of their comrades, found life in their army very discouraging. Homemade uniforms, lack of food and supplies and a long list of defeats in the closing years of the conflict, placed the Confederate "cub" in an unenviable position compared to their Union counterparts, but they fought bravely, believing they were doing their duty.

* * * * * *

The Post-Civil War Era saw the final expansion of

America in the Far West. The U.S. Army now turned to the conquest of the American Indian in a series of Indian Wars and by 1891, the Little Big Horn and Wounded Knee were history. Where were the Music Boys during this period? The Indian Wars were cavalry wars and the trumpeter was the communicator of orders on the plains and deserts of the Southwest. Ft. Laramie, Ft. Sheridan, Ft. Whipple were some of the outposts, from whence the cavalry rode to protect the settler and do battle with the Indians.

Their service as cavalry trumpeters was the finale for the Army Music Boy. In 1893, Frederick Jackson Turner, the noted historian declared that the American frontier had come to an end. His declaration also heralded the beginning of the end for Army Music Boys.

America's young soldiers fought and died alongside their older brothers-in-arms. The Southern cadets educated to be gentlemen found themselves suddenly thrown into the ranks of the Confederate Armies and wrote a new chapter in the history of American military history. The cadets at West Point, though not involved in combat, became the nucleus of leadership in the U.S. Army.

The drummer boys, fifers, and buglers were the "walkie-talkies" of an age devoid of electronic devices and often a determining factor in whether a battle was a victory or defeat, for their job was one of timing and ability. In the earlier years, the drummers gave signals for troop movements, but the practice was discontinued because it revealed the troop's position. Later, the drummer became the announcer for commands in camp and along the road of march and to build morale. The bugler was essential to the use of cavalry troops and light artillery, because these troops moved so swiftly that bugle commands did not betray their position, since moving troops were difficult for the enemy to pinpoint.

The Ponies of all of America's wars marched into battle beating their drums and blowing their fifes and bugles and trumpets. They trudged through bloodsoaked thickets, cared for the dead and the dying, and stood their ground against the enemy. They left a treasure trove of memories to their sons and grandsons. The drummer boys and bugle boys disappeared before World War I. By the time the last drummer boy and bugler had left the Army before World War I, it could be said that their predecessors had served through five wars and the first one hundred and sixty years of American history. They were in the woods of New England and the cold of Valley Force during the Revolution. They marched to New Orleans in 1812 and through the Mexican hills in 1846. They helped to lead the move West and they saw their finest moments in America's worst hours during the Civil War.

Today, the cadets at the three military academies are older; the drummers and fifers are older too, but they continue in the tradition of their predecessors which is best summed up for all of America's soldiers in the motto of the U.S. Military Academy: Duty, Honor, Country.

Notes for Chapter 1

1. M. M. Quaife, ed. "A Boy Soldier Under Washington: The Memoir of Daniel Granger." *Mississippi Valley Historical Review XVI* (March 1930), p. 540.
2. Augustus Buell. *History of Andrew Jackson* (New York: Scribners, 1904). p. 52.
3. *Ibid.*, p. 52.
4. Ebenezer Fletcher. "Narrative of Captivity." *The Magazine of History* (1929) Vol 38. No 3, p. 9.
5. Sidney Forman. *West Point* (New York: Columbia University Press, 1950), p. 25.

6. William Couper. *One Hundred Years at V.M.I.* (Richmond: Garrett & Massie, 1939), p. 295.
7. William Couper. *The V.M.I. New Market Cadets* (Charlottesville, Va.: The Michie Company, 1933), p. 5.
8. O. J. Bond. *The Story of the Citadel* (Richmond: Garrett & Massie, 1936). p. 77.
9. *Ibid.,* pp. 84-85.
10. U.S. War Department, Adjutant General's Office (Washington: Government Printing Office, 1865).
11. George T. Ulmer. *Adventures and Reminiscences of a Volunteer,* or a Drummer Boy from Maine (Chicago: Published by author c. 1892, p. 59.
12. C. W. Bardeen. *A Little Fifer's Diary* (Syracuse: W. C. Bardeen, 1910), p. 115.
13. Eben P. Sturges, Diary (21 July 1864), U.S. Military History Collection, Carlisle, Pennsylvania.
14. H. E. Gerry. *The True History of Robert Henry Hendershot* (n.d.), p. 43.
15. *The Story of the Fifty-Fifth Regiment Illinois Volunteer Infantry.* A Committee of the Regiment (Clinton, Mass.: Coulter, 1887), pp. 238.
16. *Ibid.,* p. 237-8.
17 Willard A. Heaps. *The Bravest Teenage Yanks* (New York: Duell, Sloan and Pearce, 1963), p. 90.
18. *Ibid.,* p. 92.
19. *Ibid.,* p. 63.
20. *Ibid.,* p. 37.
21. *Ibid.,* p. 59.
22. *Ibid.,* p. 59.
23. Luther Bingham. *The Little Drummer Boy* (Boston: Henry Hoyt, 1862), pp. 67-69.
24. Frank Rauscher. *Music on the March* 1862-1865 (Philadelphia: Press of William F. Fell & Co., 1892), pp. 167-68.
25. Delevan Miller. *Drum Taps in Dixie* Watertown, New York: Hungerford-Holbrook, 1905), pp. 28-29.
26. David E. Johnston. *The Story of a Confederate Boy in the Civil War* (Portland: Glass & Prudhomme, 1914), p. 130.

Fifer, 1778
Virginia Militia

Washington Visits the Troops at Valley Forge Christmas Day, 1777. Drummer Boy in Foreground. (Courtesy, The Anne S.K. Brown Military Collection, Brown University)

Cadet Francis U. Farquhar, Class of '61, U.S.M.A.
(Courtesy of U.S. Army Military History Institute) (Mollus)

Sergeant John Lincoln Clem, "The Drummer Boy of Shiloh and Chickmauga" (Courtesy, Cincinnati Historical Society)

Before and After (Courtesy, U.S. Army Military History Institute)

Col. O. Malmborg and Orion P. Howe (Drummer-boy). (Courtesy, U.S. Army Military History Institute)

Robert H. Hendershot, "Drummer Boy of the Rappahannock."
(Courtesy, U.S. Military History Institute)

VOLUNTEER ENLISTMENT.

STATE OF MICHIGAN, TOWN OF Detroit
COUNTY OF Wayne

I, Robert H. Henderson born in the City of New York in the State of New York aged sixteen years, and by occupation a Drummer Do HEREBY ACKNOWLEDGE to have volunteered this fourteenth day of August 1862, to serve as a **Soldier** in the Army of the United States of America, for the period of *THREE YEARS*, unless sooner discharged by proper authority: Do also agree to accept such bounty, pay, rations, and clothing, as are, or may be, established by law for volunteers. And I, Robert H. Henderson do solemnly swear, that I will bear true faith and allegiance to the **United States of America**, and that I will serve them honestly and faithfully against all their enemies or opposers whomsoever; and that I will observe and obey the orders of the President of the United States, and the orders of the officers appointed over me, according to the Rules and Articles of War.

Sworn and subscribed to, at Detroit this 14th day of August 1862 } Robert H. his + mark Henderson
BEFORE me Griffin Peacock
Notary Public of Washtenaw Co Michigan

I CERTIFY, ON HONOR, That I have carefully examined the above named volunteer, agreeably to the General Regulations of the Army, and that in my opinion he is free from all bodily defects and mental infirmity, which would, in any way, disqualify him from performing the duties of a soldier.

[illegible]
EXAMINING SURGEON.

I CERTIFY, ON HONOR, That I have minutely inspected the Volunteer, Robert H. Henderson previously to his enlistment, and that he was entirely sober when enlisted; that, to the best of my judgment and belief, he is of lawful age; and that, in accepting him as duly qualified to perform the duties of an able-bodied soldier, I have strictly observed the Regulations which govern the recruiting service. This soldier has dark eyes light hair light complexion, is five feet five inches high.

M. A. Hogan

8th Regiment of Michigan Volunteers (*Infantry.*)
RECRUITING OFFICER.

NOTE.—The *Oath* herein recited must be taken before a Justice of the Peace, Notary Public, or other officer authorized to administer Oaths. The *Surgeon's Certificate* following, is to be given by the Examining Surgeon, at the regimental rendezvous, when the recruit goes into camp. The Recruiting officer, in filling up the certificate at the bottom of this page, will be particular to specify the *number* of his Regiment.

Recd? M A Hogan

Robert Henry Hendershot's fictitious enlistment paper (National Archives)

General Grant's Cavalry Escort, 1865 (Library of Congress)

A V.M.I. Cadet after the Battle of New Market (Courtesy, Virginia Military Institute)

Bugler Boy, Governor's Island, 1880's (Courtesy, U.S. Army Military History Institute)

Bertram S. Flint, 16½ years. Troop G. 8th U.S. Cavalry 1898 (Courtesy, U.S. Army Military History Institute)

CHAPTER 2

NAVY

When America declared its independence on July 4, 1776, the new nation possessed no navy. The Royal Navy had been the protector of America's shores during the period prior to the American Revolution. The American Navy, a navy of privateers and states navies, was ill-equipped to do the job which lay ahead.

The Second Continental Congress appropriated money for a Continental Navy of warships, but still relied heavily on the privateers and state ships to protect American ships and ports and to harass the enemy at sea. The privateers, mostly from New England, were operated for profit, but sailed with letters of marque which came from the government ensuring their legality. The company which owned privateers was charged with supplying the captains and crews and the profits went to the owner who paid his men from the sale of goods captured by the privateers. These ships were not considered part of the Continental Navy, but a supplementary force; their chief value to the government was the damage they inflicted on enemy ships and the havoc they wrought on enemy commerce.

State navies were formed to meet their individual needs. The Pennsylvania Navy was formed for the defense of the Delaware River while the Virginia Navy was established to protect the extensive and jagged inlets and rivers of the state. The Connecticut, Maryland and South Carolina Navies sought to defend their states' coastlines and their ships rarely ventured into the open seas, but their defensive roles relieved the Continental Navy of patrolling the coastline and left them free to seek out the Royal Navy.

American children served aboard merchant and colonial naval vessels long before our nation became independent. The building of the Continental Navy and state navies saw young lads in the naval actions of the American Revolution. That event started the enlistment of very young boys in the United States Navy.

The Navy provided an adventuresome career for young boys because public education was non-existent; only the privileged received an education and often that was substandard and interrupted. The wealthy New England and Middle Atlantic merchants and shipbuilders, and the Southern plantation owners could afford tutors or local academies for their sons. The midshipmen, future officers of the Navy, had some education before they entered the naval service; the boys received most of their basic education after their entrance. Divided by socio-economic status, the boys of the upper class served as Midshipmen; the less privileged as Boys.* One thing both ranks had in common was their age, ranging from as young as eight to as old as fifteen when they began their service. The midshipmen and boys proved themselves to be brave and capable, for the times in which they lived were times of uncertainty and struggle and manhood came to them early in life. Many were "old salts" by age eighteen.

---

*Boy was a rank in the U.S. Navy; it was at the bottom just below Ordinary Seaman. To avoid confusion, since Boy (the rank) and boy (the male sex) are spelled and pronounced the same, the name Boy (the rank) will be capitalized.

I. Midshipmen

As early as 1750, sons of prominent American families entered the Royal Navy as midshipmen, including George Washington who received a warrant for service in the Royal Navy. His mother entreated him to change his mind and his decision changed history.

During the Revolution, the Marine Committee of the Second Continental Congress made the appointments and no age limit was in force. Boys as young as nine were known to be taken to sea, often the son of the captain, but in those cases, it was usually aboard privateers or on vessels of the state navies. The number of midshipmen varied according to the size of the ship, from as few as eight to as many as twenty-seven.

Often, John Paul Jones kept midshipmen aloft during the day when at sea; one each was stationed as a lookout on the maintop gallantyard, maintop gallant cross-trees, foretop gallant yard, and three kept on the quarterdeck as his aides. In the battle between the *Bonhomme Richard* and the *Serapis,* one midshipman commanded the foretop with fourteen men, another the smaller mizzen top with nine men and another stayed with Jones as his aide.

The midshipmen's uniform of 1776 consisted of a blue lapelled coat, a round cuff faced with red, stand-up collar with red at the bottom and buttonhole, blue breeches and a red waistcoat. Jones changed the naval uniform in 1777 and midshipmen wore the same uniforms as lieutenants which consisted of a dark blue coat with white linings and lapels (which the midshipmen did not have on their coats); white waistcoat, breeches and stockings. Although Congress never formally adopted the new uniform, it became the general uniform of the Navy.

Midshipmen in the Continental Navy seemed to be used primarily as prizemasters. When ships were captured, it was necessary to have them sailed into port and a midshipmen was given the task and command of the captured prize. A problem had arisen regarding captured ships called prizes. Privateers were allowed to keep all of the prize money; the Navy only one-third. This inequity was finally resolved in late 1776 when it was decided to increase the share to one-half, if it were a prize merchantman, transport or storeship and the entire value of a prize if it were a privateer or man-of-war.

Upon leaving the Continental Navy, the midshipmen received a leaving certificate, and a statement of his pay and prize money. It is believed that midshipmen received warrants ranking below a master's mate, equal to an ensign today.

There were no midshipmen in the Revolutionary War who later gained fame as outstanding naval commanders. When the Continental Navy was disbanded, the youngsters who were interested in a career at sea turned to the merchant marine. Fifteen years would elapse before the U.S. Navy came into existence.

Between the period when the U.S. Navy was established in 1798 and the War of 1812, America experienced growing pains as a nation, and became the pawn of Britain and France in their duel for control of the seas. America's struggle for naval survival during those years, produced some of the country's most illustrious naval leaders and proved a training ground for future naval heroes.

Economic conditions and aspirations for social leadership contributed to the desire of many youngsters to become midshipmen in the newly created U.S. Navy. Many of the appointments were made by no less a personage than the President of the U.S. or at least the Secretary of the Navy.

Families whose immediate ancestors had fought in the Revolutionary War had the best chance at midshipmen's warrants, both as a reward for services rendered by an older generation and hopefully as a guarantee of loyal and dedicated service by the new generation. There was a great desire to build up a strong navy although Republican sources regarded it as an unnecessary and aristocratic service.

Napoleon's desire to conquer Europe and Britain's determination to thwart his ambition, caught the United States defenseless at sea with no protection for its merchant marine which was flourishing out of Salem and New Bedford, Boston and Charleston, and contributing to the much needed prosperity of a fledgling nation. The U.S. Navy was created by an Act of Congress in 1798 and the senior officer corps of the Navy was composed of Revolutionary War veterans who for the most part had originally been trained as merchant marine officers.

The role and education of youngsters as midshipmen became a complicated matter. Alexander Hamilton, as the Inspector General of the Army, recommended a naval school for the United States and the plan was submitted to Congress in 1800. The plan also provided for a fundamental school, engineer school, artillery, cavalry and infantry school. West Point founded in 1802 included the fundamental, engineers and artillerists, but the naval school was excluded. It was believed that practical experience aboard ship was the best education a young midshipmen could receive, to learn about the sea, to study the ship at sea, and to manage men.

Schoolmasters had been authorized aboard ships in the Regulations of 1802, but no schoolmasters were employed until the War of 1812. The chaplains had the responsibility of educating the midshipmen in basic subjects, although many of the boys had already received a private education prior to their entry into the Navy.

The first school for midshipmen was established at the Washington Naval Yard in 1805 by Chaplain Robert Thompson. He conducted it aboard the *Congress,* a frigate which remained "in ordinary" or reduced commission from 1805 until 1812.

On July 23, 1806, Thompson received an order from the Secretary of the Navy to remain in Washington to instruct officers who applied for instruction in mathematics and navigation. In May of 1807, Thompson was ordered to the frigate *Chesapeake* at Hampton Roads, Virginia, to continue instruction of midshipmen in navigation. He continued to fight for the establishment of a naval academy at Washington, but to no avail, and he died in service in 1810. His successor was Reverend Andrew Hunt, a Presbyterian clergyman who ran the academy for midshipmen until 1823 serving as the one man faculty. Another chaplain, Reverend Felch established a school at Sackett's Harbor on Lake Erie in 1814 where he instructed lieutenants and midshipmen in navigation and mathematics.

The Chaplain Corps is justified in taking credit for any academic instruction which was given to the midshipmen prior to 1820 at which time the Navy gave more serious consideration to furthering the education of its future officers.

The youngsters received warrants in the Navy until after 1813 when they were required to serve at least six months satisfactorily before receiving a warrant. Pay varied from $10.50 to $19.00 a month.

Promotion was slow and depended on when a ship's regular line officer was promoted, resigned or died. Then, one of the ship's midshipmen was examined and "ranked." Midshipmen occupied a rank between commissioned officers and crew.

The midshipmen were given the nickname of "reefer" and were assigned various duties aboard ship. One was assigned to each top when the higher sails were set—from whence their nickname probably came—reefing the sails. During storms, their duty was to encourage the men by taking the most dangerous places on the yards. They had to be in the way of the seamen to see that all the needed gear was manned and no skulking was taking place, but removed themselves out of the way of the huge gangs of seamen hauling on ropes. The reefers were basically masters of the deck and messengers of the watch and it was their duty to ship and stow stores, to look after the rigging, the spars, the sails and the hold and to prepare cables for anchoring, and clear and stow them after weighing. The more experienced midshipmen served as officers of the deck and acted as clerks, and the youngest one was responsible to bring the captain's belt and pistols to him when men were called to quarters. Their duties were to ascertain the position of the ship, keep journals, acquire information applicable to their profession and to attend the instruction provided for them.

The rules of 1802 and 1815 stated:

1. No particular duties can be assigned to this class of officers. They are promptly and faithfully to execute all the orders for the public service which they shall receive from their commanding officer.
2. The commanding officer will consider the midshipmen as a class of officers, meriting in an especial degree their fostering care. They will see, therefore, that the schoolmaster performs his duty towards them by diligently and faithfully instructing them in those sciences appertaining to their profession, and that he use his utmost care to render them proficient therein.
3. Midshipmen are to keep journals and deliver them to the commanding officer at the stated periods on due form.
4. They are to consider it as a duty they owe to their country, to employ a due portion of their time in the study of naval tactics, and in acquiring a thorough and extensive knowledge of all the various duties to be performed on board a man of war.[1]

The first American naval hero who was an American midshipman at an early age was Thomas Macdonough, the hero of the Battle of Lake Champlain in the War of 1812. He received his warrant as a midshipman from President John Adams on February 5, 1800, at the age of sixteen and during the Undeclared War with France, joined the U.S. Ship *Ganges.* He went on a cruise to the East Indies in search of the enemy which resulted in the capture of two Guineamen and a French privateer.

Macdonough contracted yellow fever and was sent to a hospital in Havana, but on the way home was captured by an English ship-of-war because the merchant ship carried

Spanish cargo. He was transferred to an American ship and taken to Norfolk.

Returning from another trip to the West Indies, he arrived in America to find the Navy dismantled after the conflict with France. Soon this condition changed as the Tripolitan pirates attacked American shipping and Macdonough sailed for the Mediterranean on the *Constellation* to meet the new and additional menace to American shipping.

All four Perry brothers served as midshipmen in the U.S. Navy; two became famous and two remained unknown in history. Oliver Hazard, Matthew Calbraith, Raymond, and James Alexander Perry were sons of a naval captain, Christopher Perry who had seen service in the Revolutionary War as a youngster, first in the Kingston Reds, an elite militia company and later on privateers as a seaman. After the war, Christopher signed on as a master of a trading vessel and later became a captain. When the Undeclared War with France began in 1799, he was commissioned a captain in the U.S. Navy and given the command of the *General Greene.*

Oliver, age thirteen, was given a midshipman's warrant by Jefferson and served as a junior officer under his father when Captain Perry went to Haiti during the trouble with the French at sea. Toussaint L'Ouverture led the blacks against the mulattoes on the island of Santo Domingo and appealed to the American government for assistance. Toussaint promised in return to suppress French colonial privateers who were spoiling neutral commerce and agreed to open Cape Haitien and Port au Prince to American and British merchant ships.

Captain Perry began his tour of duty cruising around Hispaniola (Santo Domingo) to convoy American merchantmen to and from Port au Prince, but was soon ordered to the south coast of Haiti to help Toussaint capture Jacmel, the principal port held by Andre Rigaud, the mulatto leader fighting the blacks. Rigaud had a fleet of armed barges which he used to capture becalmed merchant ships. Toussaint invaded Jacmel and the *General Greene* blockaded the port and fired on Rigaud's batteries, Toussaint rewarded Perry with 10,000 pounds of coffee and since American sailors didn't drink coffee, it was sold to a local merchant for $2,000.00 and each man was given a share, midshipmen receiving $30.00.

Captain Perry came to realize that not all midshipmen were the gentlemen the U.S. Navy sought to have in its officer corps, and four on board the *General Greene* turned out to be ruffians who stole from the ship's stores, brought brandy on board and got drunk, slept on watch, fought and quarrelled and damned everything and everybody in sight. These early midshipmen, although referred to as "young gentlemen" were in reality rough and riotous and ready with their fists, and life in steerage was difficult. Food in port was good; at sea, it consisted of hard-tack often infested with weevils, tough and indigestible beef soaked in brine, squashy rice, pork and bean soup, and scouse, a mixture of hard-tack softened with water and pork fat baked together in a pan. The midshipmen received a grog ration, with the older midshipmen sneaking it away from the younger ones; a practice which led to intemperance on the part of some of the midshipmen.

Since midshipmen were not allowed to be flogged, an armchair was rigged upon the quarterdeck and the boys sat with a board around their necks, pillory-style.

This action in Haiti was Oliver's only experience in the Quasi-War with France and he went on a leave of absence when the ship returned to Newport, Rhode Island, on July 21, 1800, and spent his time at home mastering the flute and reading the classics.

As a result of the Non-Intercourse Acts and Embargo Acts passed to prevent British impressment of American seamen, Newport suffered a depression in 1809 and Captain Christopher Perry, now a retired captain, but a successful businessman, encouraged his three other sons to choose the Navy rather than the merchant marine.

The other famous Perry brother, Matthew Calbraith,

received a midshipman's warrant signed by President Jefferson and joined the Navy as a midshipman on January 16, 1809, at the age of fifteen. He reported for duty to his eldest brother on board the *Revenge,* and then in October, Calbraith and his older brother Raymond reported to Commodore John Rodgers on the *President.*

Calbraith's and Raymond's day began like any midshipman's day at dawn, when the drums sounded and the night sentries fired off their loaded guns followed by reveille and the boatswain piped and then shouted: "All hands, ahoy" followed by another pipe and "All hands up hammocks ahoy." The midshipmen continued to sleep while the men scoured down the deck; then at seven o'clock were awakened by the midshipman of the watch. While the hammock boys performed their duties, the midshipmen had their breakfast and walked on deck. Each reefer had a hammockman or cot boy from the crew to stow his hammock, take it from the nettings at night and wash it at intervals for which the reefer paid him in grog, soap, tobacco or cash. These men were the predecessors of the officers' stewards of later years.

After breakfast the drums rolled while the ensign was run up; the guard changed into a full uniform and the band played music on the quarter-deck. At nine o'clock, the midshipmen assembled in the captain's cabin or on the gun deck for school conducted by the chaplain in the earlier days; the schoolmaster in later years. Instruction was devoted to navigation for two hours and then the class moved to the spar to "take the sun" or "shoot the sun." By this procedure, the midshipmen learned to work out the last day's run and the ship's position at noon.

At noon, a midshipman presented himself to the captain and informed him of the time. A bell was struck and the boatswain and his mates blew two pipes signalling the cessation of all work. The midshipmen went to steerage for dinner while the crew ate on the gun deck. The other officers dined later, the lieutenants at one, called to the meal by the bugle which was also the signal for the crew to return to work. At four o'clock work ceased for supper which took place between four and five o'clock by all members of the ship.

Following dinner there was time for relaxation. The youngsters read, played some instruments or just idled away the time. With sunset, the drums rolled, the colors were hauled down and the night pendant was raised. The marine in undress uniform replaced those in full uniform and the band struck up "Hail Columbia." Thirty minutes later, the boatswain's whistle signalled "All hands, stand by your hammocks, ahoy!" At eight, in the winter and nine in summer, the drums signalled the end of the day. At the first roll, the bell was struck and the bugles were blown. At the second roll, the sentries discharged their day muskets and exchanged them for loaded ones. As the lights were gradually put out, a midshipman was sent to the wardroom to see that all fires were out. By ten o'clock, the officers of the watch were on duty and each half hour struck the ship's bell which was answered by the sentry's cry, "All's well; all's well."

The following incident illustrates the part played by two of the Perry brothers in the uncertain years prior to the War of 1812. Both boys were prepared for the coming conflict with Great Britain.

On April 22, 1811, the *President* was anchored off Annapolis, when word arrived from the Navy Department, that a British ship believed to be the *H.M.S. Guerriere* had been stopping American merchantmen at the entrance to New York harbor and impressing American seamen. The *President* was ordered to sail to New York immediately. Commodore Rodgers was seventy miles away at his estate at Havre de Grace. Midshipmen Calbraith Perry commanded a boat of oarsmen and they rowed all one night and most of the next day to bring Rodgers back to Annapolis and his flagship. On May 9th, Rodgers set sail and a week later, the *President* spotted a British ship at 12:30 p.m.

The British ship thought the *President* was a French ship and gave chase in hopes of a prize. Rodgers decided the

British ship was a man-of-war and at 1:30 p.m. when the strange ship reversed course and stood to the southward and showed no colors, he ordered the American ensign to be raised and called the men to their battle stations by the beat of the drum.

Rodgers was sure the strange ship was the *Guerriere,* but he found later it was a British sloop-of-war called *Little Belt.* By 7:30 p.m., not being able to make out the ensign of the other ship, Rodgers brought the *President* to a hundred yards of the Britisher and asked for recognition. The English Captain Bingham asked the same question of the American. Rodgers repeated himself, but before the answer came, a cannon shot lodged in the mainmast of the *President.* One of Rodger's gun captains returned the fire and the skirmish began and lasted fifteen minutes.

Little Belt was a captured Danish warship and although the British captain refused to surrender, the *President* ceased firing. *Little Belt's* casualties included thirteen dead and ten severely wounded. On the *President,* only a boy was wounded and Captain Bingham refused all aid offered by Rodgers to assist in the repairs. This incident was denounced on both sides of the Atlantic; Rodgers was brought before and exonerated by a court of inquiry, and the Perrys went back to Newport for leaves at home during the winter of 1811-1812.

On June 20, 1812, two days after Congress declared war, the *President* then moored in New York, received the news that the Second War for Independence had begun. Calbraith entered the following words in the sea journal: "At 10:00 a.m. news arrived that war would be declared the following day against Great Britain. Made the signal for all officers and boats. Unmoored ship and fired a salute."

Midshipman James Alexander Perry, twelve years old, was with his older brother, Oliver Hazard Perry at the Battle of Lake Erie, although he slept through the initial stages of the battle, but his brother transferred him from the *Lawrence* to the *Niagara* from whence Oliver directed and won the Battle of Lake Erie.

Probably the most interesting and most outstanding naval personality of the nineteenth century was David Glasgow Farragut, America's first admiral. The rank of admiral was not established in the U.S. Navy until the Civil War. Commodore was the highest rank prior to that period. However, in the Revolutionary War, Commodore was the courtesy title of the senior captain or officer in tactical command of a squadron or task force.

David Farragut's mother died of yellow fever as a result of nursing Sailing Master David Porter, the father of David Porter, Jr. The elder Farragut had been stationed at the New Orleans Naval Station with David Porter, Sr., and when taken ill was brought to the Farragut home, where he died. Mrs. Farragut and Porter were buried at the same time.

David Porter adopted young Farragut out of a feeling of debt to the dead boy's mother. He was appointed a midshipman at the age of nine by President James Madison, at the suggestion of Secretary of the Navy, Paul Hamilton. Farragut later said:

> Thus commenced my acquaintance with the celebrated Commodore David Porter, late of the U.S. Navy, and I am happy to have it in my power to say, with feeling of the warmest gratitude, that he ever was to me all that he promised, my friend and guardian.[2]

In August, 1811, Captain David Porter took command of the Frigate *Essex* accompanied by his ward and newly warranted Midshipman David Glasgow Farragut. Although he only stood 4'9'' tall, young Farragut was addressed as "Mr. Farragut." The crew's first glimpse of him was in his full dress uniform—a blue coat with tails, white vest and breeches, buckled shoes and a gold-laced cocked hat. His standing collar was decorated with a gold lace diamond, the insignia of a midshipman and the youngster wore a dirk at his side.

His living quarters aboard the *Essex* were in the steerage or "gun room" just forward of the wardroom. The quarters were not well lighted or ventilated and in the winter, buckets of sand buried with hot 24-pound shot, gave the reefers heat and a place to warm their feet. Farragut and his companions kept their possessions in sea chests and lockers.

One of the midshipmen's duties was to command all the boats which left the ship, including the captain's gig or wherry. Farragut's earliest experiences of command took place in Norfolk where he performed his duty with ability and determination. His extreme youth and small stature contributed to an unexpected and unpleasant event. An eleven year old boy shouting orders to men on board the captain's gig was an unusual sight to the people of this Navy town used to witnessing more mature looking midshipmen.

> . . . a handful of dock loungers espied this small boy in his blue coat with brass buttons in charge of a boatload of sailors. They began ragging, and one wag sprinkled him with an old water pot. The seaman in the bow caught the offender with his boat hook, dragged him onto the boat, and the sailors began cuffing him. The other loungers leaped forward, the crew jumped out of the boat as if decanted, and the fight moved uptown to Market Square, where the police quelled it and arrested all concerned including Mr. Midshipman Farragut, who had been dashing about in the midst of it. The result was that the midshapman and his crew were bound over by the authorities to their captain for discipline. Capt. Porter was not outraged but told his officers that young Farragut was composed of 'three pounds of uniform and seventy pounds of fight.'[3]

Just when he was becoming acclimated to life at sea, the *Essex* was ordered to Newport; Glasgow was ordered to school while the ship was in port. The way of life in 1812 demanded that children get an education when and where they could. No public school system existed, and although a warranted midshipman, Farragut was still working for a living. The deterioration of Anglo-American relations rescued him from his studies and he sailed off to war, which came on June 18, 1812.

On July 4, 1812, the national holiday was celebrated with an additional ration grog given at noon and plum pudding was served at dinner. The national ensign was flown at both the mainmast and foremast in honor of Independence Day, a happy prelude to Farragut's tenth birthday, which came on July 5th.

On July 11th, a succession of victories began for the *Essex.* She spied a convoy of seven British transports heading from the Barbados to Quebec. She captured or destroyed the *Samuel and Sarah,* the *Lamprey,* the *Leander,* the *Hero,* the *Nancy,* the *Brothers,* the *King George* and the *Mary.*

No fighting had taken place in all these captures, so Farragut's first sea fight did not come until August 13th when Porter captured the sloop *Alert* which was the first British man-of-war to be taken in the War of 1812. Farragut tells about the capture in his journal but does not mention what part he played in it. However, he does relate an interesting incident in connection with its capture in which he contributed greatly:

> I will here mention an incident which shows the advantage of exercising the men to a certain custom which I have heard severely commented on by officers of the Navy. It was the habit of Captain Porter to sound the alarm of fire at all hours of the night; sometimes he would have smoke created in the main hold. This was for the purpose of testing the nerves of the crew, and preparing them for an emergency. Whenever this alarm was given, every man repaired promptly to his quarters with his cutlass and blanket, to await the orders of the commander. At the commencement of this system a little confusion would sometimes occur, but delinquents were promptly punished, and in a short time the cry of 'Fire!' did not affect the steadiness of the men; on

> the contrary, the greatest alacrity was manifested throughout the ship on hearing the alarm, and the application of the system or the occasion I am about to relate was singularly effective.
>
> While the ship was crowded with prisoners they planned a mutiny. The coxswain of the captain's gig of the *Alert,* who was a leader in the affair, came to my hammock with a pistol in his hand, and stood by it, gazing intently upon me. Seeing a man thus armed, and recognizing him as a prisoner, I knew there must be something wrong, and, probably from fear more than anything else, I remained perfectly motionless until he passed. Then, slipping from my hammock, I crept noiselessly to the cabin and informed Captain Porter of what I had seen. He sprang from his cot, was on the berth deck in an instant, and immediately cried 'Fire! Fire!' The effect was wonderful. Instead of attempting to strike the fatal blow, the prisoners, or mutineers, became alarmed and confused, nor did they recover from their stupor until they heard the boarders called to the main hatch by the Captain, whom they now saw for the first time in their midst, to secure them.[4]

On the next cruise, which was to be a commerce-destroying cruise, the *Essex* was part of Bainbridge's squadron which also included the *Constitution* and the *Hornet.* The itinerary was to include crossing the Atlantic to the Cape Verde Islands and then sail across the South Atlantic to the coast of Brazil hence to the Pacific. Porter, Farragut and the *Essex* left on October 28, 1812. Porter appeared to be heading for Africa but changed his course and sailed southward. Around Cape Horn the ship ran into a terrible storm and lost many of her provisions. The ship then headed for Valparaiso, Chile, where the men had liberty and the ship was reprovisioned.

The *Essex* captured several prize ships, among them New England whalers which had been captured from the British and put under the protection of Peru. Among the whalers was one *Barclay* and young Farragut was placed in command of her:

> I was sent as prize-master to the *Barclay.* This was an important event in my life, and when it was decided that I was to take the ship in Valparaiso, I felt no little pride at finding myself in command at twelve years of age. . . . The Captain and his mate were on board, and I was to control the men sent from our frigate, while the Captain was to navigate the vessel.[5]

The captain of the *Barclay* was a grumpy old fellow not happy having a child in command of his ship and threatened Farragut that he would end up in New Zealand:

> I considered that my day of trial had arrived (for I was a little afraid of the old fellow, as everyone else was). But the time had come for me at least to play the man; so I mustered up courage and informed the Captain that I desired the maintopsail filled away, in order that we might close up with the *Essex Junior.* He replied that he would shoot any man who dared to touch a rope without his orders . . . and then went below for his pistols. I called my right-hand man of the crew, and told him my situation; I also informed him that I wanted the maintopsail filled. He answered with a clear 'Aye, aye, sir!' in a manner which was not to be misunderstood, and my confidence was perfectly restored. From that moment I became master of the vessel and immediately gave all necessary orders for making sail, notifying the Captain not to come on deck with his pistols unless he wished to go overboard; for I would really have had very little trouble in having such an order obeyed.[6]

In February of 1814, the *Essex* and the British ships *Phoebe* and the *Hector,* fought a naval engagement outside the port of Valparaiso, a neutral port. All three had been in port and as such had not engaged each other in conflict, but Porter decided to run the blockade. Midshipman Farragut displayed great courage and dedication to duty. He relates that he served as captain's aide, quarter-gunner and powder boy and in any other capacity that he could fill. He had his first encounter with naval casualties.

> In going below, while I was on the wardroom ladder, the Captain of the gun directly opposite the hatchway was struck full in the face by an eighteen-pound shot, and fell back on me. We tumbled down the hatch together. I say fortunately, for as he was a man of at least two hundred points' weight, I would have been crushed to death, if he had fallen directly across my body. I lay for some moments stunned by the blow, but soon recovered consciousness enough to rush up on deck.[7]

Captain Porter decided he had no alternative but to surrender the *Essex* and told Farragut to inform the officer in charge of the signal-book to throw it overboard. The youngsters collected up the pistols and threw them overboard rather than have them fall into enemy hands.

Then Farragut headed below to assist the surgeon in the care of the wounded which the future admiral described—as a scene of bloody and mutilated bodies—a scene so terrible that the youngster became faint and sick, but pulled himself together and went about dressing the wounds of his comrades. Farragut was so upset about the defeat that he cried and Captain Hillyer, the British captain called for Farragut to come and have breakfast in his cabin with Captain Porter.

The crew was paroled on shore and Farragut was engaged in caring for the wounded. He said:

> I never earned Uncle Sam's money so faithfully as I did during that hospital service. I rose at daylight and arranged the bandages and plasters until 8:00 a.m.; then, after breakfast, I went to work at my patients.[8]

In April, 1814, the American prisoners were sent back to

New York on the *Essex Junior* which had been disarmed. When Farragut returned home, he was only twelve years old.

He went to the Porter home in Chester, Pennsylvania and found a new baby in the family named David Dixon Porter, fifteen months old. Farragut attended school and studied under a man called Neff, who had been a guard of Napoleon's. Soon he was sent to the receiving ship *John Adams,* where he witnessed the chaos of youth involved with tobacco and whiskey—an experience which made a lasting impression upon him. When his squadron was ready to sail, the Treaty of Ghent had been signed and he saw no more active sea duty during the War of 1812.

Peace did not last long. The United States became involved in a war with Algiers and David Farragut was ordered to the *Independence,* the flagship of Bainbridge's squadron. On April 11, 1815, he was assigned to be aide to Captain William M. Crane. His new ship was three times as large as the *Essex* and being the captain's aide on such a large and important ship placed Farragut in an enviable position among the other fifteen midshipmen.

By June 15, 1816, the Dey of Algiers had signed a treaty with the United States which ended the paying of tribute to Algiers. Returning home, Farragut's new assignment was the *Macedonian* for a month to be followed by orders to the *Washington.* Again Farragut was chosen as the captain's aide, this time to Captain John Orde Creighton. After sailing extensively throughout the Mediterranean, Farragut went to Tunis with Chaplain Folsom who had been appointed the American Consul there. Folsom felt that the young midshipman should have the opportunity to study in a foreign city.

On his way to Tunis, Farragut spent a month in Marseilles on board the *Erie,* sightseeing and beginning his social life. He attended dinner parties and learned to play whist, and in Tunis, he studied French, Italian, English literature and mathematics.

His social life was centered around the consular corps of

the city and he was invited to be a houseguest of the Danish Consul who had a home at Carthage which proved to be of great historic interest to the youngster. His stay in Tunis was cut short by the outbreak of plague and he returned to his squadron and spent the next few years cruising in the Mediterranean and enjoying a very active social life on land. When he left Tunis in 1818 the American Consul at Tripoli wrote Folsom:

> With regard to my young friend Farragut, if he will only apply steadily to useful purposes the talents with which he is so bountifully enriched, it must, with respect and esteem of all who know him, insure him, at some future period, high in the niche of fame.[9]

In a later letter, Jones referred to David as "the young Admiral." How prophetic his words were!

Another midshipman who would later gain fame in another war, the Mexican War, was Robert F. Stockton. The future self-proclaimed governor of California entered Princeton University at the age of thirteen and stood first in his class. The following year in 1811, he received his midshipman's warrant and was ordered to the frigate, the *President* under command of Commodore George Washington Rodgers. She was soon involved in a naval battle with the British frigate *Belvidira.*

> During the action, his coolness and his fine military deportment attracted the particular attention of the Commodore. The sagacious old sea captain saw in the manly bearing of his young midshipman, the true sort of stuff—the enthusiasm which kindled with the roar of guns and the undaunted self-possession which the tumult of battle only concentrated.[10]

He was sent to Baltimore where his first assignment was to lie on the wharf and watch the enemy's moves. He continued to act as a spy and courier during the bombardment of Baltimore and led a naval infantry attack on that city in 1814. With three hundred men under his command, he marched below the city to repel the British attack on the *Lazaretto.* The enemy was thwarted, but Stockton found he was on a narrow neck of land with no boats to cross the bay. Numerous English forces were posted to intercept his retreat. He extricated himself from the enemy and placed his troops between the British and American forces.

He sent a messenger to Commodore Rodgers and informed him of the situation. The Commodore ordered him to induce an attack from the enemy before nightfall; to meet them and have them behind him.

> As soon as he received these instructions, he stationed about two of his men on each side of the road on which he intended to retreat, with directions not to fire a shot until they had the enemy between them, and, raking the other hundred, proceeded to reconnoitre his opponents. On approaching, he discovered the British encampment flanked by a thick swamp. As he was proceeding quietly and cautiously in advance of his men, he was unexpectedly fired upon from one of the enemy's outposts. Looking in the direction of the shot, he saw a British soldier reloading his musket for another trial. Stockton gave him a chance to exchange shots, and when they had both fired it was supposed to be the last shot which the Englishman ever made. This drew out the British, and a general skirmish took place. Stockton, retreating on his ambush, was followed by the enemy until they came within sight of the sailors, who, having heard the frequent reports of their comrades' rifles, could not repress their excitement. Shouting 'Stockton has got them—he'll bring them along!' disclosed themselves, when the enemy suspecting a stratagem, presently checked their advance and concluded to return.[11]

Then he went to Washington with Commodore Rodgers who consulted with the Secretary of the Navy. The midshipman acted as an aide to the Secretary for a few days and then rode at night to Alexandria to spy and report back to the Secretary of the enemy's attack on that city.

He returned to Baltimore where he towed enemy vessels and sank them in the channel near the fort with the enemy firing shells over his head. At the marine battery, he helped in driving ships from their moorings and then served as an express rider taking information from the fort to the general.

He wore the midshipman's uniform of the day which was a straw hat, blue jacket and linen trousers. The story is told that by the end of the battle his hat and jacket were gone and he was lent clothes by the general. Stockton was a master's mate by age sixteen.

Midshipmen's contributions to victory in the War of 1812 were acknowledged by Congressional resolutions which awarded swords to the nearest male relatives of midshipmen killed in that conflict and the growing importance of the Boys and midshipmen in the War of 1812 is evidenced by the legislation enacted in 1813 which directed one school master to be appointed by the captain; his pay $25.00 per month and two rations on all ships carrying seventy-four guns.

The Second War for Independence saw the end of boys under twelve being issued warrants as midshipmen. In the year 1818, every midshipman was expected to know the following before promotion: the manner of rigging and stowing a ship, the handling of artillery at sea, arithmetic, geometry, trigonometry, navigation and how to make astronautical calculations for nautical purposes.

By 1827, fourteen was the acceptable age to become a "reefer". At that age, however, he had to present evidence that he could read and write well, understand the principles of English grammar and the elementary rules of arithmetic and geography.

After the War of 1812, the need for naval schools was evident and they were established at the naval stations at Norfolk, Boston, New York and Philadelphia. The midshipmen were encouraged to attend when on shore between cruises. The most important one was at the Naval Asylum at Philadelphia founded in 1838 where the final examinations were held before being promoted to Passed Midshipmen.

Starting in 1816, there had been discussion of establishing a naval academy similar to West Point, but again many critics in the Navy felt that experience at sea was far superior to any education on land. The school for midshipmen established at the Gosport (Norfolk), Virginia Navy Yard in August, 1821, was under the charge of Chaplain David P. Adams on board the frigate *Guerriere* with Lieutenant Watson as the Superintendent of the Institution, who lived aboard the ship. The naval schools were not at first recognized by law.

The *Java* (a ship used later) and the *Guerriere* were stripped of all gear and were probably empty hulks. They were used in lieu of proper recitation rooms, drill halls, sleeping quarters and mess rooms for the midshipmen, and servants cooked and attended on the young gentlemen.

The curriculum included mathematics, astronomy, French, English grammar, naval tactics, laws of nations, Ancient and Modern History, geography, hydraulics and the use of the sword. A classical scholar was the assistant to Chaplain Adams and he was authorized to employ a French teacher and and fencing master. Ammen describes life at the Naval School in Philadelphia as very pristine:

> Our recitation room was furnished with two blackboards, and a large rough table in the centre of the room, upon which we could put our books if desired, and all of us had chairs. There was an old sextant, to explain its adjustments and no apparatus whatever. The passage-ways were heated by two stoves, placed in the middle and supplied with anthracite coal and our recitation-room was heated in like manner. Our food was paid for out of our pay, by deducting twenty dollars per month for everyone, and the wife of the gunner who was stationed as an

assistant, to take care of the pensions, was our purveyor. We did not live luxuriously.[12]

Boys had to wait until they were twenty years of age and had served five years including three years of sea duty before they were examined for promotion. If they qualified, they were ranked as passed midshipman. Two examinations and rejections were allowed before being dismissed. Passed Midshipmen received warrants as such and outranked all other midshipmen. Their pay at $25.00 per month and two rations a day set them on the course of waiting for a vacancy to open for lieutenant—a long wait, sometimes as long as twenty years.

Between the years 1828 and 1835, midshipmen on a frigate were assigned to the following positions:

1. four oldest to the forecastle had charge of the forwardsails
2. one on the main deck
3. one on the berth deck
4. one charged to watch the liquor when it was pumped into the hold.

The others were divided into three or four watches and it was the responsibility of the midshipmen of the watch to muster the men at night, to call them for their watches. The others acted as aides to the officers of the deck, as they had since the Revolution.

The lieutenant watched over the reefers who saw that they were constantly on deck and informed the captain if a strange sail was seen at night during war. Every master had a sufficient number of midshipmen observing the meridian altitude of the sun and taking double altitudes if necessary. He also used the midshipmen to help in any other calculations needed. It has been said that the duties of a midshipman were three: obeying, keeping the journals, and acquiring knowledge.

When the reefers were ashore they were stationed at recruiting establishments and receiving ships to help in caring for the men, were sent home on leave (without pay), and furloughed for duty in the merchant marine, or sent to one of the naval schools to improve the knowledge of their profession.

Memoirs of different midshipmen vary in their descriptions of life aboard ships, particularly relating to the treatment they received from their fellow midshipmen and from the officers. An example of extremism in the line of discipline was displayed by Commodore John Orde Creighton in 1829 who would muster his midshipmen in full dress uniform, and cause the ship's tailor to cut off some inches of their coat-tails because the regulations required:

> . . . short-tail coats in full dress and he allowed not the slightest license of artistic taste to the tailor in his idea of the fitness of things to the human form. Tall men and short men, lean and fat, all must have short tail coats. When "all hands" were called on the flagship, his midshipmen were required to be at their stations in the tops or elsewhere in full tog—cocked hats, swords or dirks, and must be trig and neat in person. On one occasion one of the midshipmen, a brusque, burly youngster, who stammered in his speech, was going aloft to his station in the maintop, when the Commodore's keen eye espied a hole in his coat under the arms. Hailing the main rigging he asked in loud, sharp tone, why he was going aloft with his coat torn under the arms; the stammering quick reply of the reefer: 'Well, Co-commodore, what's a fe-fellow to do when to-other coat's torn?' brought as quickly its well-merited punishment.[13]

Midshipman Benjamin (later Admiral) Sands, like Farragut, had a memorable experience in commanding a boat which left the ship. He observed a squabble in the bow of the boat and

> . . . saw blood upon the white trouser of our bow-oarsman who, in getting us into a berth to await the return of the stewards with their marketing, had pushed a Portuguese merchantman's boat with his boat-hook, when its keeper drew his knife and

> stabbed him. My boat's-crew jumped ashore to capture the man who did the stabbing, and a cry was immediately raised by the sentinel for the guard who came double-quick to the scene. My men, being unarmed, seized oars and boat-hooks to make fight, when I got between the belligerents and succeeded in getting my men into their boat and shoved off, having in the meantime seized the man and passed into their boat. One of my men seized the musket of the sentinel and threw it overboard. Fortunately, neither party used arms, I, having wholly forgotten the long uniform dirk hanging at my side, did not use it, and the sergeant of the guard displayed great forbearance, or there would have been more blood shed, and it would have been the worse for us.[14]

David Dixon Porter, America's second admiral, began his unofficial career as a midshipman at the age of eleven. He had gone to sea with his father in December, 1823, in an unofficial capacity where he was treated like a midshipman and learned the rudiments of a sailor's routine. This experience ended in February of 1824 and although short in duration, it set the course of David Dixon's future—officer, U.S. Navy.

He spent two years at Columbia College in Washington where he studied English, the classics and mathematics, but during this period, his father, David Porter, was court-martialed for the Fajardo Incident.

This action by the Navy was the result of an incident which had occurred in Puerto Rico. A young naval officer had gone ashore at Fajardo and had been insulted by the mayor and other authorities. Captain Porter reacted by going ashore with a large company of seamen and forced the Spaniards at gun point to make an abject apology which he dictated to them.

The Monroe Doctrine had been issued a year before and the Administration in Washington feared Spain would declare war as a result of Porter's actions. Porter was recalled and an inquiry ordered, thinking Spain would protest. Nothing was forthcoming from Spain and the hearings were postponed.

New England Congressmen and some newspapers attacked Porter. He felt his honor was at stake and demanded that Secretary of the Navy Samuel Southard convene the board to either clear him or dismiss him from the Navy. The board met early in May of 1825. To complicate matters, Commodore James Barron was to be a member of the board; Porter had served on a court-martial board that had tried Barron in 1807 and voted against him.

The inquiry started with Porter villifying Southard; he was asked to retract his statements and he not only refused, but walked out of the room. Southard retaliated by ordering a court-martial. The verdict of the court suspended Porter for six months. However, he was completely exonerated for his conduct in Puerto Rico, and after six months of contemplation, Porter resigned from the U.S. Navy and accepted the command of the Mexican Navy with the rank of capitan de navio (not admiral as he had hoped).

Young David Porter's official career began as a midshipman in the Mexican Navy at the age of thirteen. His first ship was the flagship, the *Libertad* on which he first sailed in 1827. He was rated a midshipman on the *Esmeralda* under the command of his cousin, Captain David Henry Porter, where he helped put down a mutiny. The Porters commanded a skeleton crew to sail the ship home.

The following year, the *Guerrero* was attacked by the Spanish frigate of sixty-four guns, the *Lealtad.*

> Midshipman David Dixon Porter sprinted along the smoky length of the ship from quarter-deck to forecastle to shriek Henry Porter's orders to Lts. Williams and Vanstavern. Dodging flying splinters, leaping over corpses, and wounded men and pools of blood that dotted the deck, swerving clear of the recoil of guns, he shuttled back again to his station beside the captain to receive other messages. He darted down the gangway under the rumbling deck to the magazines with a word for the quartermaster

> and the swearing Mexicans who heaved the rounds of ammunition to the gunners. He ran to the fore-mast to have the boatswain's mate card the shredded rope's ends, and splice the rigging. He was hit once by a spent ball and bruised but he was too excited to feel anything but exultation in his first battle.[15]

Due to Captain David H. Porter's maneuvers he was able to get away, but pursued by the *Lealtad,* Porter decided to surrender; he was killed before he could negotiate with the enemy.

David Dixon Porter was captured and placed on a guard ship in Havana Harbor where he was later exchanged and sent home at age fifteen. In 1829, he entered the U.S. Navy as a midshipman at sixteen and was assigned to the *Constellation,* the flagship of the Mediterranean squadron.

His experience in the Mexican Navy had made him more qualified than many senior lieutenants in the American Navy and his ego and cockiness were resented by many of his shipmates. He played tricks on other midshipmen who looked up to him, and after some reluctance on the part of senior officers, he was granted his warrant. His future success was predicted by Commodore James Biddle, commander of the Mediterranean squadron who wrote in his report to the Navy Department that "Midshipman D. D. Porter will become an officer worthy of the name he bears."

Prior to the Civil War, duelling was commonly practiced and many of the midshipmen took part in this practice. In 1830, Alexander M. McClung and Addison C. Hinton stole ashore in a market boat at Montevideo and wounded each other in their duel. Sands' description of what actually happened illustrates the tensions which arose in steerage:

> Some days prior to the duel he [McClung] sought a quarrel with Midshipman Williams who was quietly seated on our side of the steerage. McClung walked over to my locker and taking therefore my long dirk or uniform dagger, he put it into his bosom. . . . Soon afterwards he went over to where Williams was sit-

> ting conversing with his friends, and leaning forward he made some very offensive remark, of which Williams, evidently not wishing to have any difficulty, did not take notice at first, but, glancing up, he saw the hilt of the dirk protruding from McClung's vest, and he immediately seized it, and threw it up the hatchway overboard near where he was seated; but before the two could come to actual blows their messmates got between them, preventing a collision.[16]

Besides widespread duelling, obstreperous midshipmen became a problem to many captains. Many young midshipmen fainted at the floggings inflicted on the enlisted men (a practice not used on the midshipmen), but individual punishments were decided upon by different captains. Captain John Orde Creighton of swallowtail fame knocked Midshipman John Matson down with his speaking trumpet.

When Calbraith Perry was twenty years old at the end of the War of 1812, he married into the Slidell family and became a brother-in-law to Alexander Sliddell, an eleven year old whom Oliver Hazard Perry appointed acting midshipman. Several years later, Slidell added Mackenzie to his name and was the captain of the ship associated with the most unfortunate incident in U.S. Naval History which involved midshipmen.

Commodore Perry was a champion of the apprentice system* and assigned the new ship *Somers* to be an experimental schoolship for the youngsters. He chose his brother-in-law Master Commandant Alexander Slidell Mackenzie to be her captain. Lt. Matthew C. Perry, Jr., twenty-one, served as acting master and Oliver H. Perry II, seventeen, served as captain's clerk and was appointed acting midshipman once the ship was underway. Henry Rodgers, the younger son of the commodore, was also a midshipman on the *Somers.*

The Secretary of War at the time was John Canfield

---

*The apprentice system will be discussed later in the chapter.

Spencer whose son, Midshipman Philip Spencer, nineteen, was also assigned to the ill-fated crew. He had a history of expulsions from Hobart and Union Colleges and on his first assignment which was the *U.S.S. North Carolina,* he had struck Passed Midshipman William Cravey twice. Although a serious offense, Perry ignored the report to the Navy Department. Assignments to other ships included incidents of drunkenness and reports of planned mutinies. His commanding officers feared the administration in Washington and Secretary of the Navy Upshur assigned him to the *Somers* where Mackenzie, knowing his record, refused him.

Spencer unshaken by the action, went to Commodore Perry who intervened and had the midshipman returned to the *Somers,* where 70 percent of the crew was under nineteen, a perfect breeding place for trouble led by a juvenile delinquent. There were seven midshipmen aboard, four between sixteen and nineteen and of seventy-four apprentice boys, twenty-two were under sixteen; the rest young enough to be considered minors.

Two of the crew, a Samuel Cromwell, thirty-five, and Elisha Small, thirty, were the catalysts for Spencer's mutiny. The former was a boatswain's mate and senior petty officer; the latter, captain of the main top; both had served on slave ships prior to joining the Navy and were familiar with piratical procedures.

The first cruise of the new ship with Spencer on board was to the West African coast looking for slavers. Spencer immediately followed his usual pattern of behavior—neglect of duties, unfriendliness towards messmates, but friendliness with the boys and the enlisted men who broke the rules by giving the boys forbidden items of tobacco and brandy.

The ship reached Tenerife in the Canary Islands on October 8, 1842, and arrived in Monrovia, Liberia, November 10th. She then set sail for St. Thomas in the Virgin Islands hoping to reach New York by Christmas. On the cruise home, it became noticeable that Cromwell, who had formerly hit the apprentices, began currying their favor and on November 25th, Spencer took the purser's steward

Wales to the booms where in the presence of Small, he unfolded his sinister plan.

The officers of the ship would be killed. Spencer would capture the *Somers* and make it a pirate ship. Spencer, Cromwell, Small and the steward Wales, if he agreed, would be the key members of the conspiracy. The mutinous midshipman said he had a list of the "certain" and "doubtful" among the crew, and those who were unwilling would be thrown overboard to the sharks.

Wales was loyal to his captain and got word to him through his immediate superior, Purser Heiskell. Mackenzie refused to believe the plot, but on evidence that Spencer had been having conferences with Cromwell and Small, called the recalcitrant midshipman to his quarters and confronted him with the accusation. Spencer admitted to the Wales story, but added that it was just a joke. Mackenzie did not buy his ploy and had the midshipman arrested, took his sword and had him handcuffed and chained to the bulwarks. He was properly fed and covered with an officer's clock during the rain squalls.

Midshipman Rogers searched Spencer's sea chest and found the paper listing the names for "certain" and those "doubtful" and assigning posts during the mutiny. Cromwell and Small were arrested and chained. There were no marines on the *Somers* and no brig.

Tension was mounting on board, and four more suspects were arrested and chained to the bulkwarks of the quarterdeck on November 30th. The four wardroom officers and three senior midshipmen were ordered to deliberately study the evidence and advise the captain as to the disposition of the case. It was agreed that the three ringleaders be executed. An Act of Congress in 1800 stated: "If any person in the navy shall make or attempt to make any mutinous assembly, he shall on conviction thereof by a Court Martial suffer death." Although not a court-martial, Mackenzie was pressed with a mutinous element in the crew.

The execution was carried out swiftly and the men were

hanged from the yardarm. Funeral services followed with Captain Mackenzie officiating at the rites. He returned to New York where a court of inquiry was convened and he was exonerated; he then demanded a court-martial and the same decision was reached by the panel of his peers, but there were many who felt he was a murderer, among them James Fenimore Cooper and fellow officer Robert F. Stockton. The subsequent bad publicity resulting from this affair adversely affected the apprentice system since it was felt future apprentices might run the risk of being hung by a "Queeg"-type captain.

By 1841, it was realized that some knowledge of steam engines would be helpful and in 1843 a reefer was required to know how to station a crew, make arrangements for battle, exercise at quarters and use signals. Determination of rank also required that a knowledge of French, Spanish and drawing be presented. Although officers and petty officers helped the midshipmen, they learned more about seamanship from the older and more experienced sailors.

A naval school was founded on the banks of the Severn River at Annapolis, Maryland, in 1845, when the old Army fort named Severn was turned over to the Navy for the school. This action of Congress, along with the efforts of the Secretary of the Navy George Bancroft and Lieutenant Matthew Fontaine Maury, resulted in the establishment of the U.S. Naval Academy.

Its first students were drawn from the body of the midshipmen then in the Navy aboard ships, and in 1851, the four-year course was put into operation for youngsters new to the Navy.

George Dewey entered the U.S. Naval Academy at Annapolis at the age of fifteen, having passed the entrance exam which consisted of reading, writing and arithmetic. Sixty boys entered the class of 1854, fifteen graduated, among them Dewey. He had not achieved high enough rank by the time of the Civil War to be in the category of an outstanding leader at that time, but fate reserved his place of glory for the Spanish-American War when he became the

Hero of Manila Bay.

Midshipmen were younger during the period 1776-1845 and had more sea experience than the boys who went to the U.S. Naval Academy. Samuel Barron appointed at the age of two, reported for duty at eleven; L. M. Goldsborough received his warrant at seven and reported at eleven. There were many fourteen and fifteen year olds at Annapolis in the years from its founding until 1874, and some were as young as twelve and thirteen.

Confederate Midshipmen

When the War of the Rebellion began in 1861, the Confederacy was faced with the problem of training young officers for its infant navy. Many Annapolis-trained officers had joined the Confederate Navy, but junior officers were scarce.

On March 16, 1861, the Confederate Congress authorized the President to appoint as many midshipmen as he deemed necessary and set the maximum at 106. Many of the boys were sons of naval officers. The school started operations in May of 1863 aboard the partially armored steamer *Patrick Henry* in the James River. The Confederate Naval Academy was geared for a career service rather than for immediate service in a river and harbor war in which the Confederate Navy was a beleaguered landlocked navy, but the boys who served as midshipmen were considered to be very able and knowledgeable.

John Thompson Mason who had been a "marker" in the Alexandria Co. 17th Virginia Infantry, a veteran of the First Battle of Manassas, was appointed a midshipman. Aboard the *Patrick Henry,* he served at Drewry Bluff and then went aboard for service on one of the Confederate cruisers running the blockade at Charleston, South Carolina.

Life for the Confederate reefer was fraught with feelings of divided loyalties and uncertain realities. One such youngster was James Morris Morgan who entered Annapolis at fifteen in September of 1860. When his home state of Louisiana seceded, he left the U.S. Naval Academy to join the Confederate Navy. His description of his departure from the service of the U.S. is a poignant portrait of the mental turmoil which many youngsters were suffering at the time:

> As we passed through the old gate opening into the town, the gate I was not to pass through again until my head was white, fifty years afterwards and as we walked along the street, Captain Rodgers (his captain) kindly took my hand in his, and then for the first time I realized that I was no longer in the navy, but only a common and very unhappy little boy. But the Confederacy was calling me and I marched firmly on. That call seemed much louder at Annapolis than it did after I reached my native land.[17]

He was accepted in the Confederate Navy as a midshipman and forced to wear his blue uniform which caused people to stare at him in disgust. To counter his embarrassment, he had a gray suit tailored for him which he wore until the Confederate gray uniforms arrived and Morgan relates:

> In those days all the naval officers wore the blue uniform of the United States Navy which they had brought South with them, and they kicked like steers when they were afterwards compelled to don the gray, contemptuously demanding to know, 'Who had ever seen a gray sailor, no matter what nationality he served?'[18]

The *C.S.S. Alexandria* was built in Britain and Morgan was sent to spend the winter in Liverpool. He was lonely because he was the only Confederate midshipman in Europe at that time but while there he received $40.00 per month and attended nautical school to learn navigation and boating. Morgan served on Confederate ships in the bayous of Louisiana, wandered to other Confederate ships after the fall of New Orleans, and served at Drewry's Bluff in

Virginia.

The day of the young midshipman as part of the complement of ships began to disappear as the youngsters reported to the Naval Academy. Here, they would form a professional officer corps—a naval aristocracy which still exists today. Midshipmen on board sailing vessels, and the sailing vessels themselves, both became a part of naval history. They served each other well and wrote a romantic chapter in naval warfare.

II. Boys

When the Continental Navy was formed, at the begnning of the Revolutionary War, young boys enlisted to serve aboard the ships including the *Independence* and *Lexington,* the *Ariel* and the *Bon Homme Richard.* The ships averaged from nine to twenty-five boys depending on the size of the ship. During this period of the Revolution, the boys served as cabin boys except in combat, when a boy was quartered to each gun to carry cartridges. Sometimes they were drummers or fifers and occasionally they were assigned to the sick bay and ranked as loblolly boys.

The process of enlistment was a loose arrangement as the regulations were not specific and, where specific, enforced in a loose manner. The captains of many of the privateers took their sons to sea as cabin boys. Elias Hasket Derby, whose fleet of privateers made up a large part of the Massachusetts Navy, employed boys as young as eight who shared in the bounties of the ships captured from the British. Since his ships averaged six boys, four received three-quarter shares each, and the two lower ranking boys received one-half share each.

Andrew Sherburne entered the naval service at thirteen during the Revolutionary War and served aboard the *Ranger* along with twenty-nine other boys mostly from Portsmouth, New Hampshire, where the *Ranger* was built, and John Paul Jones took command. His *Memoirs* reveal that the boys became proficient in swearing and boxing and waited on the officers, but also shared in the bounty prizes.

The Pennsylvania Navy had boys as young as eight who were listed as privates, but often did not pass muster because of their sizes. A marine, age twelve, named Alexander Henderson, served on the *Dickinson* along with William Murray, a fourteen-year-old drummer, and the *Montgomery* boasted a drummer of fourteen; the *General Washington,* a boy of ten.

The Virginia Navy listed young boys on their ships and privateers and Connecticut, Maryland, and South Carolina Navies followed a familiar pattern. The youngsters were carried as "Boys" and listed at the end of the muster rolls just below Ordinary Seamen.

The Navy was disbanded after the Revolution and we do not hear about the Boys again until the Navy Department was officially established in 1798 for the purpose of countering the attacks of Napoleon's navy against American shipping. Regulations set down specified the enlistment of young boys in the naval service but did not state any age, and boys served in the U.S. Navy during the "Undeclared War" with France. John Hoxse described service aboard the *U.S.S. Constellation* in his book *Yankee Tar* where he relates that during an encounter with a French national ship of fifty-four guns, *Le Vengeance,* two Boys, John Baptist and Philip Smith, were seriously wounded.

In 1807, the U.S. Congress authorized the President of the United States to enlist a number of able seamen, ordinary seamen and boys not exceeding 500, should he find this action necessary in light of the imminent national emergency (impressment of American seamen). Two years later, Congress further authorized the President to increase the number of all the ratings to 3,600 and to 300 midshipmen to serve for a period not to exceed two years.

During the War of 1812, the Mexican War and Civil War, the boys served mostly as "powder monkeys," carrying the powder from the magazine to the guns—a dangerous job.

Monkey was a sailor's term applied to any small object, and was derived from the little monkeys on board as pets.

Samuel Leech served as a boy in the Royal Navy, and was captured by the Americans before finally joining the U.S. Navy as a powder boy:

> It was my duty to supply my gun with powder. . . . A woolen screen, saturated with water, was placed before the entrance to the magazine, with a hole in it, through which cartridges were passed to the boys. We received them there and covering them with our jackets to prevent sparks from prematurely exploding them, hurried to our respective guns. These precautions are taken to prevent the powder taking fire before it reached the gun.[19]

Leech also describes the dress worn by sailors in the era of 1814 when boarding of ships, particularly during the Algerian War in 1815:

> We were all supplied with stout leather caps, something like those used by firemen. These were crossed by two strips of iron, covered with bear skin and were designed to defend the head, in boarding an enemy's ship, from cutlass strokes. Strips of bear skin were used to fasten them on and, having the fur on, served the purpose of false whiskers and causing us to look as fierce as hungry wolves.[20]

After the war, boys continued to be enlisted for a two-year period until 1837. In 1824, the first attempt was made to establish an apprentice system. Senior officers in the U.S. Navy and members of the Congress were concerned because so many foreigners enlisted in the Navy. Secretary of the Navy Samuel Southard suggested, and Senator Robert Hayne of South Carolina introduced legislation that legal authority be granted to enlist boys. They were to be over thirteen and under sixteen years of age with their parents' written consent and to serve until they were twenty-one. It took from 1824 until 1837 for the plan to become a reality, even though such men as Lt. Matthew C. Perry and Lt. David G. Farragut championed the plan.

Congress was dubious about so many young boys associating with older men and its approval was held up because of the workings of Congress and its doubtful members.

Lieutenant Perry sent the plan to Secretary Southard in January 1824, who agreed to have between fifteen and thirty apprentices in every naval yard, and one for every gun on vessels in service. He expected the boys would qualify for the rank of ordinary seaman within two years and as seaman within three years. Perry and Southard felt the boys would have honest employment, there would be a decrease in crime, and the Navy would be built up with native-born Americans. The drawback to the two-year period of enlistment employed at the time was the loss of the boys just after they had learned the basic rudiments, and a continued career at sea was often with the merchant marine.

Lieutenant David G. Farragut established a school for apprentice seamen on board the receiving ship *Alert* at the Gosport Navy Yard in Portsmouth, Virginia, in 1826 with a class of thirty-seven boys and received great compliments from Southard. The plan did not receive the necessary support, and Southard resigned as Secretary of the Navy, but upon his return to Washington in 1833, as a Whig Senator from New Jersey, he introduced a bill to provide for the enlistment of boys in the naval service. Finally, passed by both houses on March 2, 1837, the bill took thirty-two months for passage—a measure recommended nine years before!

The Apprentice System in the pre-Civil War period differed in some ways from the postwar period. In the early years, the system itself was in the apprentice stage. Between 1839 and 1844, about 1,500 apprentices were enlisted in the Navy, but the program turned out to be a disappointment because many of the boys thought it would earn them a commission as midshipmen. Sometimes boys by special letter from the Navy Department were to be treated as midshipmen, but were to receive only Boy's pay.

Thirteen was the minimum age in 1837; in later periods it was raised and lowered; raised to fourteen in 1855, lowered to thirteen in 1865; raised to fourteen in 1870, raised to fifteen in 1875, and returned to fourteen in 1880. Besides the written consent of the parent or guardian, no boy could have physical disabilities, poor health or a criminal conviction. Some boys were orphans and in the case of the orphan boys from Girard College in Philadelphia, the Guaranty Savings and Trust Company of that city signed the consent forms. No candidate was accepted who could not spell with a fair degree of accuracy, words of two, three and four syllables, write legibly and answer questions from the multiplication tables.

The Boys were rated as Second or Third Class Boys, depending on their age, size and qualifications. The Third Class Boys received $5.00 per month, the Second Class Boys $6.00 and, when promoted to First Class, $7.00 per month. No money was issued to the boy until discharged, except for clothing and necessities and liberty expenses. The allowance was twenty-five cents a week if there were no marks against them. Four postage stamps and necessary stationery were provided monthly. The concern for the morality of the boys is illustrated by the American Seaman's Friend Society which published *Sailors' Magazine & Naval Journal* monthly and had a section called "The Cabin Boy's Locker." The November 1830 issue (when boys were enlisted rather than apprenticed as after 1837) contained a story which emphasized the "fruits of disobedience, the need for honesty, compassion and understanding and set a value on the smallest morsels of knowledge, plus the remarkable proof of the immortality of the soul." It was hoped this section would serve as an inspiration to the boy sailors. Regulations varied at different times as to the allotment of money to parents. From 1837 until 1876 it was encouraged; in 1876 it was not permitted. By 1869, one-tenth of the monthly pay was retained until the expiration of the enlistment.

An Apprentice Fund, made up from sales of all articles constituting the "ship's slush fund," the commutation for grog, and the undrawn rations, was used for the purchase of books, periodicals and newspapers, fresh vegetables and fruits, poultry and other fixings for the Christmas and Thanksgiving Dinners, and any necessary articles for the amusement and health of the apprentices. Each sailor had a "ditty bag" containing a pair of scissors, a thimble, some linen thread, a paper or two of needles, a lump of wax, and various trimmings such as tape, buttons and strips of binding.

Prior to the regular assignment of a schoolmaster to ships and prior to the establishment of the apprentice system in 1837, the chaplains were charged with the instruction and care of boys in their teens, midshipmen and Boys.

The ship's schoolmaster, selected by the commander of the apprentice-vessel was paid at the rate of schoolmasters of first rates. The ratio was one schoolmaster to every fifty apprentices. Orthography, reading, writing, arithmetic, geography and English grammar made up the curriculum of a basic education. The schoolmaster's uniform consisted of a coat of plain blue cloth, single breasted, rolled collar, and made according to the prevailing fashion for the citizens at the time, with six navy buttons on each breast, one on each hip and one on the bottom of the skirts.

There was no regulation uniform for sailors until the 1840s at which time they were authorized to wear a blue woolen frock with white linen or duck collars and cuffs, or blue cloth jacket and trousers, blue vest when vests were worn, black hat, black handkerchief and shoes in cold weather; in warm weather it consisted of a white frock and trousers, black or white hat, black handkerchiefs and shoes. The collars and breasts of the frocks were to be lined or faced with blue cotton cloth, stitched with white thread or cotton. (*The Navy Rules and Regulations of 1799* provided that poverty-stricken seaman could be supplied with slop-clothes by the order of the captain after the vessel had commenced her voyage. Uniforms for seamen were make-shift outfits.)

> Blue is the working dress of the navy; white its 'holiday rig.' Your true man-of-war's man is very

particular about his clothing. Infinite pains have been taken to give his tarpaulin that marvelous gloss. His spotless white ducks set tight about the hips and hung loosely at the bottom, just allowing the tips of a pair of patent-leather pumps to peep out from beneath their ample breadth! See him with his blue collar turned back over his broad shoulders, exposing a manly and well-turned neck; his hat pressed jauntily over his left eyebrow; one hand carelessly resting on his hip and you would scarcely need to be told that a true "blue jacket" was before you.[21]

The religious instruction, under the jurisdiction of the chaplain, took place on Sunday from 1:00—2:00 p.m. The Protestant Church teachings predominated, but were not enforced on boys of a different sect or religious persuasion. The spirit ration was not given to the boys, but they received 60 cents a month instead and were encouraged to abstain from both liquor and tobacco.

The apprentices were separated from the older men by the maintenance school ships at the principal Navy yards, but the idea failed because the boys were exposed to the bad example of some of their sailor teachers and other sailors of the Navy. In addition, they saw service on regular navy ships once they had learned the rudiments of being a sailor.

Apprentice Charles Nordhoff, who later wrote *Mutiny on the Bounty,* described the receiving ships as:. . .old vessels dismantled of their guns and laid up, in the larger seaports, to be used as temporary places of deposit for sailors whose ultimate destruction is some vessel just being fitted for sea and not ready to receive her crew.[22]

He described discipline as being very lax and life as monotonous. Some boys deserted and Nordhoff found the general atmosphere rowdy:

. . .the scenes of drunkenness and riotous debauchery of which I had been a witness almost constantly

> since my entry into the Navy could not fail of being highly disagreeable to the feelings of a lad like myself who had been raised among religious people.[23]

He was assigned to a man-of-war as a messenger boy whose duty it was to "strike the bell" every half hour and to act as errand boy for the officers.

In time of battle, he was a powder boy at gun number 36 and he had a hammock number, a ship's number and a mess number. He found that the boys were not treated with much kindness on board ship, particularly on a man-of-war.

Nordhoff was stationed in the mizzen-top where he described his delight in being stationed there:

> My life in the top was a very happy one. I was relieved of the drudgery of running errands, striking the bell, and lounging about the quarter deck, at the momentary call of the officers. I was top man and what more flattering to a boy than to be ranked among men even if he is at the 'tail of the heap.'[24]

He made the observation that only the "idlers" on the ship did not keep watch; the purser, surgeon and assistant, the chaplain, the captain and lieutenant of the Marines, the cooks and servants.

The men resented the sauciness and indifference of the boys, and the officers did not enforce the duties of the boys. There were forty boys aboard, eight on the quarter watch, four on the fo'c'sle and twelve messenger boys. All were under the charge of the master-at-arms. They were in their hammocks by 8:00 p.m.; no talking after 9:00 and mustered at 7:00 a.m.

The better educated boys had the better chance to become a midshipman. This was true prior to the establishment of the Naval Academy, as well as in the period when a very few apprentices were appointed to the Naval Academy—10 out of 500—and many boys deserted. By 1845, Secretary of the Navy George Bancroft reported that the apprentice plan had not been a success. In 1855, a new

Secretary revamped the program, just in time to provide boys for the Civil War which began six years later.

Boys, one with rank of landsman, received the Naval Medal of Honor in the Civil War. Daniel Harrington, born in 1848 in Ireland, held the rank of Landsman on board the *U.S.S. Pocahontas* and participated in a shore mission to procure meat for the ship's crew. While returning to the beach, the party was fired upon from ambush, and several men were killed or wounded. His citation read:

> Cool and courageous throughout this action, Harrington rendered gallant service against the enemy and in administering to the casualties.[25]

Oscar E. Peck, a fourteen-year-old Second Class Boy, won his medal for action on board the *Varuna* on April 24, 1862. He acted as a powder boy of the after rifle during an attack on Forts Jackson and St. Philip. The *Varuna* was attacked repeatedly and rammed and finally sunk. Peck served gallantly during this close range action.

John Angling, a sixteen-year-old Cabin Boy U.S.N., served on board the *U.S.S. Pontusac* during the capture of Forts Fisher and Wilmington on December 24, 1864. Recommended for gallantry for carrying out his duties faithfully during this period, his Medal of Honor was awarded for his cool courage under the fire of the enemy throughout the many actions.

James Machon, Boy U.S.N., also sixteen at the time of his heroism, served on board the *U.S.S. Brooklyn* during successful attacks against Fort Morgan, rebel gunboats and the ram *Tennessee* in Mobile Bay on August 5, 1864. Although wounded and sent below for treatment, he immediately returned to his post and took charge of his gun. The enemy action returned heavy fire while James Machon performed his duties with ability and courage. Again wounded, he was totally disabled.

The naval apprentice system had been revived again in 1864 by Secretary of the Navy Gideon Welles. This time, the actual training system which was to set the tone for the postwar apprentice system, came into existence. The *Sa-*

bine, the *Portsmouth*, and the *Saratoga*, old sailing vessels, were commissioned as apprentice ships. In June 1868, Congress passed an act limiting the number of enlisted men and apprentices to 8,500, so only one ship—the *Saratoga*—was necessary for their training.

The naval apprentices enlisted at naval rendezvous or on board receiving ships and were sent to the nearest naval Apprentice-ship. In 1862, U.S. Receiving Ships were located at Portsmouth, New Hampshire, Boston, New York, Philadelphia and Norfolk, Virginia. The Apprentice-ship *Saratoga*, at New London, and the *Sabine* in New York also received enlistees.

When the apprentice arrived at the Apprentice-ship, he visited the ship's barber under the direction of the master-at-arms who then had the boy wash, bathe and dress in his new uniform. The uniform had either been given to him as a gift from his parents or had been paid for by the boy out of monthly deductions from his pay. The next stop at the sailmaker provided him with his hammock and bags, hammock clews and lashings, and bag lines. Necessary needles, thread and tape were issued monthly and paid for out of the Apprentice Fund.

The apprentice then went to the mast where the executive officer assigned him to his mess quarters and station on the ship by giving him a written slip of paper. His last act before his new life began was the packing of his civilian clothes and depositing them with the master-at-arms for storage.

The boys were divided into two watches: starboard and port; into divisions of guns for great-gun exercises and drills; and into guns' crews of seventeen. The most trustworthy, capable and deserving apprentice was selected as "apprentice boatswains mate" to act as adjutant at all military functions. First and second captains of crews of great guns were chosen according to merit and fitness from the apprentices and appointed "petty officers."

The great gun's crew constituted a boat's crew for drill and exercise. The gun's crew also consisted of the mess of the apprentices. Five minutes before the meal, the meal-call sounded by drum or bugle, and the gun crews assembled, mustered and reported. Boys were chosen to be cook and assistant for a week. Their duties were to bring the food to the table and apportion it out under the direction of the first captain:

> The Mate of the deck will inspect the tables after being spread; any boy having an unfair proportion of bones, or a smaller quantity of food than the others may exchange with the Captain of the mess.[26]

Two sailors with the rate and pay of seamen were assigned to teach the boys to cut, make and mend clothes and to perform their respective services at a small charge. Two shoemakers taught the boys cobbling. Some apprentices also were chosen to learn the carpenter's trade under the direction of the carpenter and his mates by repairing boats, making boats and other spars and in carpenter's work on board ship.

By use of the rotation system, five percent of the boys received instruction in sailmaking, and five percent as boatswains. Four first class apprentices acted as signal boys for periods of two weeks and used a glass to assist in making and reading signals.

As mentioned before, one of the main functions of the young boys in the Navy was that of a powder monkey; gunnery and howitzer drill were of great importance. In the post-Civil War period, the powder monkey's job was more than just bringing the ammunition from the magazine; they learned to sponge, load, point, dismount the gun and to know the detail of cartridges, shells, fuses, primers, firing, shift breechings and how to secure a lower-deck gun. They became accustomed to the use of powder through frequent target practice and knew how to land on shore with rifles and howitzer and to operate the pivot gun. In battle, the powder boy was furnished with a leather bucket, having a tight fitting lid; in this bucket he carried the cartridges from the magazine hatch to his gun. The boys were also trained in the use of cutlasses, pistols and single sticks. (When the vessel was in port, the boys stood at the side to do honor to officers going away or coming on board and kept the side ladder clean.)

There were three departments of instruction:

1. *Seamanship*, which consisted of knotting and splicing, handling sails; handling spars and yards; sailmaking; anchors and chains; marlin-spike work; pulling and sailing boats; signal, compass and steering, lead and log lines and swimming.

2. *Gunnery* included the calls to and at quarters, the stations and exercise at great guns, knowledge of ammunition and magazine, broad sword drill, howitzers and machine guns; infantry instruction, squad drill; school of the soldiers, company drill, target firing, skirmish drill and bugle instruction.

3. *English* instruction covered reading, writing, arithmetic, spelling, geography, United States History and History of the Navy, writing from dictation, religious and vocal instruction.

On Mondays, Tuesdays, Thursdays and Fridays the schedule included naval training, brightwork and school. On Wednesdays, school was not held, but personal affairs were tended to. The schedule on Saturdays allowed leave and there was church on Sunday. Each day naval training and brightwork was on the schedule. School ran from 1:00 to 4:15; dinner was at noon, supper at 5:00, and bed at 9:00. Amusement was limited to reading, dancing and music for which the boys were provided bats, balls, skates and boxing gloves.

Punishment depended upon the offense. It varied from solitary meals to denied recreation hours, cancellation of leave, extra watches, suspension of monthly allowance, and confinement to bread and water not to exceed five days.

After the Civil War, the apprentice system declined because of the lure of the West. The adventure of the sea romanticized during the era of the clipper ships and whaling boats was replaced by the dreams of going West to find gold, fight Indians and punch cattle.

On April 8, 1875, another apprentice training system was set up by the authority of the original 1837 act. No hope of becoming an officer through the system was raised, but as inducements, apprentices were awarded badges of merit and in 1888 Rear Admiral Theodorus Bailey instituted the Bailey Medal to inspire apprentices to greater effort in acquiring a knowledge of their profession.

Four apprentice ships, the *Minnesota* at New York, the *Constitution* at Philadelphia, the *Monongahela* at Baltimore, and the *Saratoga* at Norfolk, were the training ships for the apprentices both in port and for cruises. The favorable reports about the boys when transferred to the cruising vessels led to an act of Congress in 1879 which authorized the annual enlistment of 750 boys between fifteen and eighteen to serve until they were twenty-one. Two boy heroes gave added prestige to the capability of youths.

1. John Lucy, a Second Class Boy, was awarded the Medal of Honor for action in 1876 when he displayed "heroic conduct while serving on board the U.S. Training Ship *Minnesota* on the occasion of the burning of Castle Garden at New York on July 9th."

2. In 1879, John Hayden, a sixteen-year-old apprentice won the Navy Medal of Honor for heroism on the *Saratoga*:

> On the morning of 15 July 1879, while the *Saratoga* was anchored off the Battery in New York Harbor, R.L. Rokey, an apprentice fell overboard. As the tide was running strong ebb, he not being an expert swimmer was in danger of drowning. David M. Buchanan, apprentice, instantly, without removing any of his clothing, jumped after him. Stripping himself, Hayden stood coolly watching the two in the water, and when he saw his services were required, made a dive from the rail and came up alongside them, and rendered assistance until all three were picked up by a boat from the ship.[27]

In 1883, the apprentices finally obtained a permanent

training station at Coasters Harbor Island, off Newport, Rhode Island, and after the Spanish-American War in 1899, a training station for apprentices was established on Yerba Buena Island in San Francisco Bay.

Apprentices of ability and good conduct were trained as buglers, carpenters, sailmakers and blacksmiths and, with the exception of the buglers, were assigned to their respective gangs when sent to their assigned ships.

The buglers held a solitary assignment. Bugler apprentices were required to be proficient in ship's calls; boat calls, army calls and skirmish calls. Apprentices who were trained as buglers were detailed to ships to perform this duty, but did not receive the pay of a bugler if still serving his term of service as an apprentice.

Although the boys were not exposed to the grueling work of day-to-day and hand-to-hand fighting as in wartime, boys suffered from disease and drowning, and the Navy also had the additional burden of desertions in foreign places. Walter G. Blair, a First Class Boy, deserted in Panama in 1885, and other boys deserted in such faraway places as Rio de Janeiro, Yokahama, Cherbourg, France, and William A. Dunning, a Second Class Boy, died at sea on board the *Wabash* at fifteen.

The closeness and comradeship of the boys toward one another are vividly described after the death of one of their shipmates:

> Had Charlie Smith died far off at sea his hammock would have been his casket, and the ocean his grave. Now military honors were to be accorded him. From admiral to man or boy in the Navy, of most inferior rating, nothing is wanting in medical skills and attendance in time of sickness, and, in case of death, in respect and honor to the dead...
>
> Early next morning the boys sent a petition to the executive officer to permit them to contribute toward the purchase of a handsome casket. The request was readily granted, and that evening all that was mortal of Boy Smith, in bright new uniform,

> rested in a beautiful casket—the tribute of the boys' affection for their little shipmate. Every boy was in tears as he took a last look at Charlie as he lay in state upon the gun deck, and never did a sadder ship's company go to its hammock when the drum that night beat tattoo...
>
> Silently the crew mustered on the starboard side of the gun deck. The chaplain taking his position at the head of the casket, when the order to uncover, proceeded to read a portion of the impressive burial service of the Church of England.
>
> The boats had all been lowered...the colors of each boat were half-masted. The first boat received the music and the firing party and pulled off to head the procession; next came the steam cutter with the casket, followed by the boat containing the pall-bearers.
>
> At the cemetery the military formation was broken and the boys without order were permitted to gather around the grave...the gloom was only broken by lively strains of the band as the boys marched back to the boats.[28]

The Navy Regulations of 1896 provided that a boy could obtain his discharge through purchase. It had to be done during the first eighteen months of enlistment, and the price of the discharge during the first three months was at the whole amount of pay from the date of enlistment to date of discharge; during the fourth month, thirty percent of one year's pay; during the fifth month, thirty-five percent, and so on, increasing five percent per month until the eighteenth month when the price reached a full year's pay. Amount for clothing were also deducted.

Many boys served aboard ships as buglers during the Spanish-American War, but the role of the powder monkey had disappeared with the appearance of the heavy guns of the new Navy. Purchase and tackle carried the charges of 250-525 pounds and replaced the powder monkey.

The apprentice system, much more successful in its last

stage, greatly reduced the number of foreign seamen in the Navy. By the time World War I started, the apprentice system was on its way out. The apprentice symbol was worn proudly by many sailors as late as World War II.

The apprentice system had provided a means of support to thousands of young boys and given them more education and travel than the average American boy of the period. It enabled boys to prepare themselves for careers in the Navy, the Revenue Cutter Service, or the merchant marine. The Naval Apprentice System provided a foundation for three boys who later gained fame in the civilian world. Along with Charles Nordhoff, another future author Herman Melville found his naval service a useful background for his famous work, *Moby Dick*. Naval service also proved to be a great benefit to Theodore Thomas, who enlisted in the Navy as a musician second class at the age of fourteen in 1849, and later became the conductor of the Chicago Symphony.

* * * *

The role of children in American Naval History was an important one. Although they did not fill positions of policy and decision, they contributed greatly to the overall success of the American Navy at home and abroad, at sea and at shore stations.

The midshipmen, the hope and future of the Navy formed the foundation upon which the officer corps grew in strength and stature. Most of America's naval heroes in the nineteenth century began their careers as midshipmen whether they entered as early as nine like Farragut or as old as Stephen Decatur at nineteen. They not only acted as naval commanders but in many instances were the men who carried out America's foreign policy—David Porter's subjugation of the pirates in the Caribbean, Decatur's defeat of the Barbary Pirates and Stockton's conquest of the Mexicans in California were examples of the triumph of the nation's foreign policy.

It is interesting to note that John Barry, whom many historians consider "the Father of the American Navy" came to America in 1755 at the age of ten as a cabin boy. From Barry, the cabin boy to Dewey, the midshipman, America's naval heroes began their careers as youngsters. The famous "old salts" have their special niche in history, the names of thousands of unheralded boys who "went down to the sea in ships" also deserve a place on the honor roll of American Naval History.

Notes for Chapter 2

1. U.S. Navy Department, *Naval Regulations of January 1, 1815*, pp. 68-69.
2. Loyall Farragut, *The Life of David Glasgow Farragut* (New York: D. Appleton & Co., 1882), p. 11.
3. Charles Lee Lewis, *David Glasgow Farragut* (Annapolis: U.S. Naval Institute, 1941), p. 25.
4. Farragut, pp. 16-17.
5. *Ibid.*, pp. 25-26.
6. *Ibid.*, pp. 26-27.
7. *Ibid.*, p. 41.
8. *Ibid.*, pp. 44-45.
9. *Ibid.*, p. 71.
10. Samuel John Bayard, *A Sketch of the Life of Commodore Robert L. Stockton* (New York: Derby & Jackson, 1856), p. 15.
11. *Ibid.*, pp. 20-21.
12. Daniel Ammen, *The Old Navy and the New* (Philadelphia: J.B. Lippincott, 1891), p. 95.
13. Benjamin F. Sands, *From Reefer to Rear Admiral* (New York: Frederick A. Stokes, 1899), p. 124.
14. *Ibid.*, pp. 24-25.
15. Richard S. West, Jr., *The Second Admiral* (New York: Coward-McCann, 1937). p. 25.

16. Sands, pp. 36-37.
17. James Morris Morgan, *Confederate Reefer* (Boston: Houghton, Mifflin, 1917), p. 33.
18. *Ibid.*, pp. 52-53.
19. Edgar Stanton Maclay (from the diary of Samuel Leech), *A Youthful Man-O-Warsman* (Greenlawn, New York: Navy Blue Co., 1910), p. 139.
20. *Ibid.*, p. 140.
21. Charles Nordhoff, *Nine Years a Sailor: Being Sketches of Personal Experience in the U.S. Naval Service* (Cincinnati: Moore Wilstack & Baldwin, 1866), p. 130.
22. *Ibid.*, p. 31.
23. *Ibid.*, p. 212.
24. *Ibid.*, p. 35.
25. 93rd Congress, First Session, The Committee on Veterans' Affairs, U.S. Senate. "Medal of Honor Recipients 1863-1973." (Washington: Government Printing Office, 1973), p. 111.
26. U.S. Navy, *Regulations and Routine of Drills, Exercises and Studies on Board Apprentice-Vessels* (Washington: Government Printing Office, 1859), p. 9.
27. "Medal of Honor Recipients," p. 344.
28. H.H. Clark, *Boy Life in the United States Navy* (Boston: Lothrop Publishing, 1885), pp. 159-62.

John Paul Jones bidding farewell to the *Bonhomme Richard* from the deck of the *H.M.S. Serapis.* Note "Powder Monkey" to his right. (Courtesy, U.S. Naval Academy

Midshipman 1777 (Courtesy, U.S. Naval Historical Center)

Midshipman David G. Farragut (Courtesy, U.S. Naval Historical Center)

Farragut Discovers a Man-O-War (Courtesy, U.S. Naval Historical Center)

Midshipman's Uniform 1830-1841 (Courtesy, U.S. Naval Historical Center)

Midshipman Pendleton Gaines Watmough (Courtesy, Pennsylvania Historical & Museum Commission, Hope Lodge)

Midshipmen, U.S. Navy 1852-1855 (Courtesy, U.S. Naval Historical Center)

Midshipman James M. Morgan C.S.N. Age Fifteen
(from his book, *Rebel Reefer*)

"POWDER MONKEY" standing by a 100 pounder Parrott rifled gun aboard the *U.S.S. New Hampshire* off Charleston, S.C., during the Civil War. (Library of Congress)

First Class Boy John W. Watson on *U.S.S. Constitution* at Newport, R.I., circa 1863-65. (Courtesy, U.S. Naval Historical Center)

Philadelphia, on the 23rd day of August, 1853

Witness my hand and seal: Fanny Lauba [L. S.]

Sworn and subscribed before me, this 25th day of April, 1866,

W. W. Dougherty J.P. Alderman. [L. S.]

* To be filled with the name of the Parent or Guardian.

Enlisted at Philadelphia May 4th, 1866

J. C. Howell
Commanding Rendezvous.
Comdr.

I, Theodore Lauber, having been enlisted as a Naval Apprentice, do solemnly swear (or affirm) that I have never voluntarily borne arms against the United States since I have been a citizen thereof; that I have voluntarily given no aid, countenance, counsel, or encouragement to persons engaged in armed hostility thereto; that I have neither sought, nor accepted, nor attempted to exercise the functions of any office whatever under any authority or pretended authority in hostility to the United States; that I have not yielded a voluntary support to any pretended government, authority, power, or constitution, within the United States, hostile or inimical thereto. And I do further swear (or affirm) that, to the best of my knowledge and ability, I will support and defend the Constitution of the United States against all enemies, foreign and domestic; that I will bear true faith and allegiance to the same; that I take this obligation freely, without any mental reservation or purpose of evasion; and that I will well and faithfully discharge the duties of the service which I am about to enter: So help me God.

Theo Lauber

Sworn and subscribed in presence of

J. C. Howell
Recruiting Officer.

U. S. Naval Rendezvous Comr
May 4th, 1866

No.

May 29th 1866

U. S. S. Sabine School for Apprentices.

Teachers' Certificate of Examination.

IT IS HEREBY CERTIFIED, That Theodore Lauber of Reading, Pa aged thirteen years has passed a satisfactory Examination upon all points required by the Regulations.

The following is his standing in the several branches upon a scale of 8:

Reading, 6 Writing, 6 Arithmetic, 4

[illegible] Jr
Ex. Schoolmaster.

(National Archives)

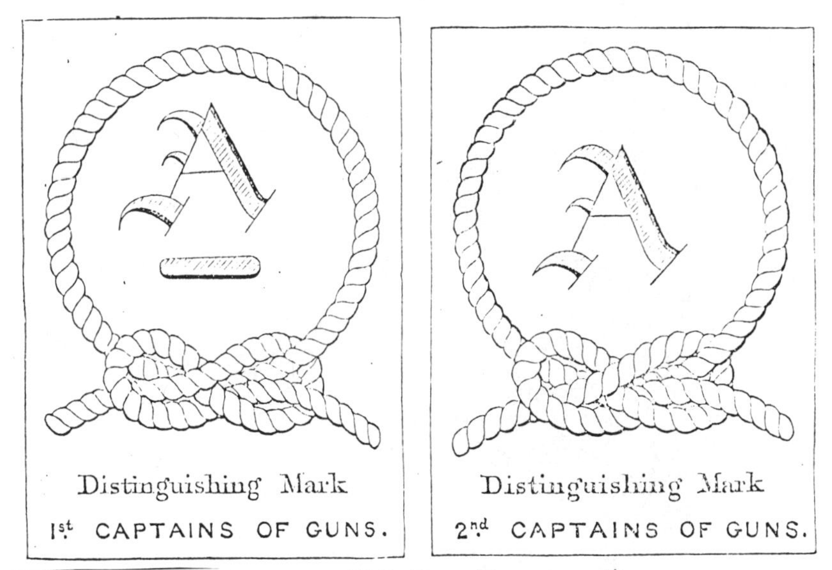

Apprentice Ranks (Courtesy U.S. Navy Department)

Apprentice Buglers, *U.S.S. New Hampshire,* 1888 (Library of Congress)

CHAPTER 3

THE U. S. MARINE CORPS

America's march king, John Philip Sousa, was born in Washington, D.C. where his father, Antonio Sousa, was stationed as a member of the U.S. Marine Band. Although surrounded by the glamorous activities of the band and life at the Marine Barracks, John Philip wanted to join the circus at the age of thirteen.

His father obtained permission from the leader of the band and young Sousa was enlisted as an apprentice in 1868. By this action, he became a part of a system which has existed officially since the corps was established in 1798, and most likely was a part of the Continental Marines.

Although no evidence exists of Marine drummer boys in the Revolutionary War, it is likely that youngsters who were the drummers used to "drum up trade" in the recruitment of Continental Marines at The Conestoga Wagon owned by Samuel Nicholas in Philadelphia which was a central recruiting point. Since Marines were the drummers and fifers aboard Revolutionary vessels, the duty was most likely assigned to the boys.

On 1 February 1799, the Commandant of the Corps, Major William Ward Burrows, wrote to Lieutenant Jonathan Church that he enlist young lads to be taught music and have them pay for their lessons and their uniforms out of their own money. He made clear the manner in which they were to be taught: "a Suit of Drummers or Fifers Clothes by the time they have worn them out, they will know how to take care of the Clothes the Public allows them. I would prefer their being taught by Note than by Ear."[1]

In June of 1800, the Commandant wrote to Lieutenant John Johnson to recruit two or three boys not exceeding age twelve, with their parents' consent to be drummers and fifers. In 1805, one of Commandant Burrow's last acts as Commandant was an instruction to Captain John Hall, the Marine officer on the *Constitution* to enlist fourteen good musicians for the Marine Corps from the Italian populace. The story is told that he landed a sergeant's guard at Catania, Sicily, and impressed a band of eighteen strolling musicians, families and all. By the time they arrived in America, the Marine Corps had a new Commandant, Franklin Wharton, who was furious at Captain Hall, and refused to allow the Italians in the band.

The foreigners formed their own group, but disbanded a year later and promptly enlisted in the Marine Band. Among the boys was Venerando Pulizzi, twelve, who served for the next forty-seven years, ending his career as a Sergeant Major at Marine Headquarters. Many of the Italians in the band were appointed as masters to the apprentices in the band. Among the young boys enlisted at Catania were Manuel Caruso, ten; Ignazio, nine; and Paitano Sardo, ten.

In 1807, Wharton wrote to the same Lieutenant Johnson, whom Burrows had contacted in 1800. This time, the Commandant mentioned that he was paying the expenses of the boys and suggested that the lieutenant place the Boy Sardo (whom Johnson had recruited) under the drum major and have him serve until he was twenty-one.

Although no other information indicates it, Commandant Wharton in a letter written on 12 June 1807 stated that he took the charge and responsibility of the enlistment of Boys as "my Apprentices or Servants." Whether this means that he also used boys who were not musically talented as servants is left to conjecture. He did state, however, that "you (Johnson) must well recollect that it was because I knew we could not secure Music for the Corps otherwise, and was therefore willing to incur an expense even by the future maintenance of those Boys."[2]

The same year Commandant Wharton set down in a letter to Lieutenant Newton Keen the requirements for indenture to be a Music Boy in the Marine Corps. Bound until twenty-one, he would be given $500 at the end of the enlistment. Although Commandant Wharton seemed to prefer boys about twelve, he stated that any age or size would be acceptable. There is much evidence this was the case.

All music apprentices were assigned to the Marine Barracks in Washington for their musical training and were then sent to various duty stations and ships. The exceptionally talented ones were assigned to the Marine Band in Washington, which explains why Sousa never saw duty with the Marine Corps other than in the capital city.

The boys served in all the wars, although they were usually aboard ships. When the Marines landed, however, they accompanied them. The boys acted as fifers and drummers aboard ship and held the same position in the field being known as the field music section.

When Marines were needed to participate in combat, a battalion or other size unit would be formed of men from one or more barracks. The field musicians would also come from the various barracks.

William Graham, a drummer enlisted in 1801 at the age of 12 and served during the War with Tripoli. Private David Coleman, 16, served in the War of 1812 aboard the *John Adams.* Private Samuel Coridell was 13 when he served as a drummer in the War with Algiers in 1815. Five boys were present at the Battle of Bladensburg during the War of 1812 when a detachment of Marines was sent from the Marine Barracks in Washington to meet the British on their approach to Washington.

When the Marines were engaged in amphibious operations, a fifer and drummer accompanied them. The following description of Marines occupying San Francisco during the Mexican Wars bears out this fact:

> The sailors in their white frocks and pants, black hats and shoes, and the Marines in their dress uniforms, led by one fifer and one drummer, marched to the customhouse in what is now Portsmouth Square, San Francisco.[3]

Music Boys went ashore with Commodore Matthew Perry in Japan in 1853. (See picture at end of chapter.)

Music Boys accompanied Marine detachments in the Civil War; twenty-one boys were at the First Battle of Bull Run in 1861; one boy, John R. Johnson was attached to the Army and four of the boys deserted in the midst of the battle.

The Panic of 1819 had a great effect on the American people. The second phase of the Westward Movement began as the Austins led Americans into Texas. The economic severity of the times made a strong impression on the poor and they sought security for themselves and particularly for their children. Their boys who sought apprenticeship in the Marine Corps often lied about their ages and in reality were several years younger than stated on the enlistment papers. The parents and guardians were anxious for their boys to finish their apprenticeship in the Marine Corps in order to have them enter into a trade.

Of twenty-one boys enlisted between late December 1825 and late March of 1826, only four were reported fit for duty. One lad, George Farwell whose age was listed as seven, was probably four and could not report for duty because of his inability to dress himself completely. Four boys listed as eight years old were probably six, and it took two of the boys of this group a year and a half to two years to be reported fit for duty with the fife and/or drum.

Private William Brown of Swanstown, Franklin County, Vermont, was six-year-old when indentured for a period of fifteen years, and re-enlisted in 1827, rated as "Drummer." James Cubkner, nine-year-old, stood only three feet eight inches tall when he enlisted to learn music, and was rated Fifer in 1829. Another six-year-old, Eppippam Tuasy, was ordered by the court to enlist for thirteen years with the consent of his father. Their titles varied over the years from Musics to Music Boys to Boys Learning Music. In the latter part of the nineteenth century, there averaged about twenty-five boys at headquarters in Washington. The number increased to forty in 1904, and in 1916 there were sixteen.

One eleven-year-old, Theodore Cuvillier, did no duty except to play the horn at private balls and serenades. His father was a good bassoon player in the U.S. Marine Band and received his son's pay as a tip for his talents.

The young boys were apprenticed to senior members of the Marine Band. The indenture papers made it very clear that they were to learn "the art, trade and mystery of a musician." All the rules were stated in the indenture papers and the responsibilities of the master were clearly defined. The boys were forbidden to play cards or dice, to enter into matrimony, to frequent taverns or gaming places, or to drink or swear, and were admonished to be good and faithful apprentices. The masters' duties included providing food, drink, clothing, lodging and other necessities.

Later in the century, the age limit was raised to fourteen for entrance. The boys were required to attend school twice a day to learn bugle calls and drum rolls, and also received an ordinary school training. Their instructors were paid four dollars a month out of each boy's monthly pay. The boys were permitted to go on leave every Wednesday, Saturday, Sunday and holidays, until rated either a trumpeter or a drummer. Once rated, they enjoyed the privileges of the men. The trumpet replaced the fife toward the end of the century, because it became impossible to hear the fife in the noise of battle.

The Marine Music Boys were as prone to the antics of youngsters as any other boys. As evidence of early disciplinary problems, Commandant Wharton wrote to Captain Thomas R. Swift on 1 November 1816:

> I have a Boy here, who, most vicious is, without friends and I am not willing, by turning him into the world, at his age, to expose him to certain ruin, but will make one more attempt to save him. He has been to a degree taught the Drum, but wants practice; put him under Secore, and see what you can make of him; he's here too well known, and his habits too bad to expect a change; perhaps you may be able to mend him, by your advice and discipline. I shall send him to you with a hope of success.[4]

As late as 1912, they were found to be guilty of smoking, insolence, stealing, being absent without leave and insulting the sentry. The punishments varied from extra duty as a painter to two days on bread and water; loss of liberties to five days on bread and water; loss of pay to ten days of confinement. Life in the barracks is well described in the following account:

> In the old barracks here in Washington I've seen from sixty to eighty apprentices out at the crack of dawn for reveille; about half of them were fifers and the rest were drummers. There was also a big bass drum that was beaten on both ends and made a terrific noise. For fifteen minutes they marched around the old quadrangle playing, "The Breaking of the Day," "Hearts of Oak," "Gary Owen" and "Blue Bonnets Over the Border." You had to be an early riser to live in the neighborhood of the barracks; there was no sleep after our fife and drum corps got warmed up to their work.[5]

Many of these music boys served aboard ships in the Spanish-American War and two were killed on the *U.S.S. Maine*: John Henry Dierking, Drummer from Brooklyn, and Charles H. Newton, Fifer of Washington, D.C.

An illustration of the life of a Marine Music Boy is that of

Sergeant Major Christian Steffens who joined the Marine Corps in 1894 at the age of fifteen in New York. His rank was Apprentice Field Music. Sent to the Brooklyn Navy Yard, he was issued blankets, given a meal and bed to spend the night. The following morning, the boys were taught the facing movements in drill and given a rifle to learn the manual of arms. The training lasted from three days to a week before being put on duty.

Upon completion of his recruit training, he was sent to the Field Music School in Washington, D.C. as a drummer. He also had to learn to play the bugle, which included memorizing 105 different Garrison, Field and Ship's bugle calls. Two years later, Steffens was rated a drummer and stayed in the capital for two years before receiving his first assignment aboard a ship, which came in 1898 when he was ordered to the *U.S.S. Lancaster.*

John R. Bailey joined the Marine Corps at the age of fifteen in September 1915. Upon completion of his course, he was rated as trumpeter in June of 1916 and was assigned to the Marine Barracks at Norfolk. He was home on furlough when his assignment to the U.S. Legation in Peking, China, arrived. Due to his absence, he did not go to China, but was later assigned as trumpeter on the new battleship *U.S.S. Pennsylvania.*

As already mentioned the best known Music Boy of the Marine Band was John Philip Sousa who re-enlisted as a Third Class Musician in 1872 and was Leader of the U.S. Marine Band by the time he was twenty-six. The rest of his career in the Marine Band and in the world of music is history.

Notes for Chapter 3

1. National Archives Record Group 127 Letters Sent Aug. 1798-June 1801.
2. *Ibid.*, March 1804-Feb. 1884.
3. K. Jack Bauer. *Surfboats and Horse Marines: U.S. Naval*

Operations in the Mexican War 1846-1848. (Annapolis: U.S. Naval Institute, 1959), p. 155.

4. National Archives, 1804-1884.
5. Harold C. Reisinger. "Andrew Mealey and the Mongoose." *The Marine Gazette*, vol. 25, no. 4, February 1931, p. 41.

MARINES WITH COMMODORE PERRY IN JAPAN IN 1853. Note drummers and fifer in upper right hand corner. (Courtesy, U.S. Marine Corps Historical Center)

William Crawford, Fifer, USMC, age 13. Photo taken at time of enlistment, Washington, D.C. 1866. (Courtesy, Military Music Collection, U.S.M.C. Historical Center)

Millard F. Smith, age 14; Marine Corps full dress; entered U.S.M.C. in D.C. as a bugler and drummer; stationed at Dry Targuas, Fla.; circa 1895. (Courtesy, U.S. Army Military History Institute)

Music Boys in the 1890's on board the *U.S.S. Massachusetts.* (Library of Congress)

Field Musics, U.S. Marine Corps, 1900 (Courtesy, U.S. Marine Corps Historical Center)

Music Boys at the Marine Barracks, Washington, D.C. 1916 (Courtesy of Miss Elizabeth Koller)

I, John Philip Sousa

do acknowledge that I have voluntarily enlisted myself to serve 7 years 5 months 27 days in the Marine Corps of the UNITED STATES, unless sooner discharged, upon the terms mentioned in the act passed the 11th day of July, 1798, entitled "An act for establishing and organizing a Marine Corps:" also the act passed the 2d day of March, 1833, entitled "An act to improve the condition of the non-commissioned Officers and Privates of the Army and Marine Corps of the United States, and to prevent desertion:" also the act passed the 30th day of June, 1834, entitled "An act for the better organization of the United States Marine Corps:" also the act passed the 2d day of March, 1837, entitled "An act to provide for the enlistment of boys for the Naval service, and to extend the term of the enlistment of seamen:" also the act passed February 20, 1845, entitled "An act to amend an act entitled "An act to provide for the enlistment of boys for the Naval service, and to extend the term of the enlistment of seamen:" also the 9th section of an act passed March 3d, 1845, "making appropriations for the Naval service for the year ending the 30th of June, 1846:" and also the 3d section of an act passed 12th June, 1858, "making appropriations for the Naval service for the year ending the 30th of June, 1859:" and that I have had read to me the Rules and Articles of the Army and Navy against Mutiny and Desertion.

Witness my hand, this [illegible] day of June 1868.

IN THE PRESENCE OF—

Saml Miller [illegible]
2nd Lieut U.S.M.C.

John P. Sousa

I, John Philip Sousa,

do solemnly swear or affirm, (as the case may be,) that I will bear true allegiance to the United States of America, and that I will serve them honestly and faithfully against all their enemies or opposers whatsoever, and observe and obey the orders of the President of the United States, and the orders of the officers appointed over me, according to the Rules and Articles for the government of the Army and Navy of the United States. And, further, that I am of the age of [illegible] years [illegible] months and [illegible] days.

John P. Sousa

Sworn before me, at [illegible]

this [illegible] day of June 1868.

C. P. Porter,
2nd Lieut & Adjt.

SIZE ROLL.

John Philip Sousa a boy, born in the Washington D.C. State of [illegible] County of [illegible], Town of [illegible] enlisted [illegible] June 1868 at [illegible] for 7 years 5 months 27 days, by [illegible] aged 13 years 6 months 3 days, 4 feet 9 — inches high, black eyes, black hair, dark complexion, by trade or occupation a Cabinet maker

REMARKS.

I CERTIFY, *That the above recruit is free from bodily defects, and is qualified to perform the duty of a soldier.*

L. J. Williams
Surgeon

Apprentice Papers of John Philip Sousa, U.S.M.C. (National Archives)

CHAPTER 4

QUASI-NAVAL SERVICES OF THE UNITED STATES

The year 1789 not only heralded the beginning of our nation under the written Constitution, but it also marked the establishment of the Lighthouse Service to be followed the next year with the creation of the U.S. Revenue Marine Service. These two services, along with the Life-Saving Service founded in 1847, were incorporated into the U.S. Coast Guard in 1915, the year in which the services were beginning to phase out children in their ranks.

It is necessary, therefore, to account for each of the earlier services separately and although not considered armed services in the strict sense, there were many exploits of bravery performed by children. In the Revenue Marine (later Revenue Cutter Service) the youngsters who held the rating of Boy in this service faced the same dangers as

America's sailors when the Revenue Marine was ordered to duty with the U.S. Navy, as well as the dangers involved in law enforcement on the seas and in ports which were the prime functions of the service at that time.

Alexander Hamilton is considered the father of the U.S. Revenue-Marine and its birthdate of 1790 makes it the oldest of all the services, but has the least amount of information as regards the role of young boys in the service. Evidence is clear that youngsters served on board ships from its establishment.

Congress authorized twenty boys at four dollars per month, two boys per cutter. At this time, there was no age limit for enlistment of boys so it is probable they ranged in age from nine years on as was the practice in the Navy at that time. By 1799, the boys were earning five dollars per month. It is not clear what their duties were, but it is likely they served as cabin boys and/or deckhands. Since there was a total of only six seamen including the boys (the other four hands were known as Mariners), they probably served in any capacity in which they were needed.

However, during the Quasi-War with France, Captain George Price of the U.S. Revenue Cutter *General Greene* received the following communication from the Secretary of the Navy (under whose jurisdiction the service was attached during the emergency):

> The Crew of the Cutter *General Greene*, under your command, may consist of fifteen Able Seamen, Ten Ordinary Seamen, Five Boys and Ten Marines. . . .[1]

Evidently, the number of Boys was increased with emergencies.

In the War of 1812, two boys, John Bowden and Edward Page were listed as Lads on board the Revenue Cutter *Surveyor* which was captured by the British in the York River in Virginia. The captain, Samuel Travis suspected the British frigate *Narcissus* was in the fog-shrouded vicinity and he ran out his own guns and sent a patrol boat to give warning. The boats met three boats from the frigate with fifty men under the command of Lieutenant John Crerie. Amidst shots, the Americans escaped, but with the sound of the shots, Travis issued two muskets to each of the fifteen men on the cutter. The British boarded the vessel and Travis was forced to surrender. The two lads were among the prisoners who were captured. Lieutenant Crerie admired the bravery of the Americans who were greatly outnumbered by the British and soon paroled the boys.

The only reminiscence of a Boy in the Revenue Marine Service is that of Samuel Samuels who joined the Revenue Cutter *Jefferson* at Mobile, Alabama in 1826 at the age of thirteen. He relates that he signed on for six months at $18.00 per month (which is doubtful) but deserted after several months. He was so inadequate or inept as a deck hand that he was made the coxswain of the captain's gig. If his tales are true, it is evident the service was not run in a very military fashion and since the *Jefferson* patrolled the waters of Mobile Bay it turned out to be very monotonous duty for an adventuresome boy.

By 1834,the uniform for the Boys consisted of a blue jacket with a white frock collar and facings of blue; a star on each side of the collar; two stars on each of the breast; and "white or blue trousers" according to the season, with blue belt.

In 1834, the regulations of the service mention that Boys would be paid six to ten dollars per month and one navy ration. The regulations of the Revenue-Marine issued in 1843, states that two Boys would be considered as equivalent to one seaman, and the pay would be the same as in 1834. It also states that no Boy could be enlisted under thirteen, or under four feet nine inches, and parental consent was necessary. By 1894, fourteen was the minimum age, and there was a probationary period of two months, and remained so until World War I when the age was raised to seventeen.

In 1871, the regulations made it clear that the Boys' duty was in the officers' messes or as buglers. This was a departure from the Navy's policy of no servant roles for the boys.

Although classed as First, Second, or Third Class Boys, Revenue Cutter Service boys were called wardroom boys, cabin boys, or buglers. The pay scale of 1881 gave First Class Boys in the Pacific $17 per month, and those in the Atlantic and Great Lakes $15.

There were five Boys on the great ice ship *The Bear* when it sailed to Alaska in 1897; the ship later became famous for her rescues and patrols. The First Class Boys were paid $17.00 per month and three Second Class Boys received $15.00 per month.

The Revenue Cutter Service followed the Navy's practice of having the youngsters serve as buglers. Below are the bugle calls which the Boys were required to know on shipboard in 1898:

> Reveille, Sick Call, Recall, The Call, Clean Brightwork, Secure Gig, Three Flourishes, Knock off Brightwork, Secure Launch, Morning Colors, Drill Call, Secure Cutter, Tattoo, Officers' Call, Secure Whale or Surfboat, Taps, Assembly, Secure Dingy, Hammocks, General Quarters, Secure Admiral's Barge, Mess Gear, Commence Firing, Hook On, Mess Call, Cease Firing, Dismiss, Silence.

The best known boy of the service was Charles Jones Soong, a member of the service on the *Gallatin* at the age of sixteen. Five feet tall at the time, his name first appeared on the muster list in January 1879. He served as a cabin boy to the captain of the cutter, Eric Gabrielson of Edgartown, Massachusetts, and re-enlisted for another year of service when his first hitch expired. This time he served aboard Gabrielson's new command, the *Schuyler Colfax.*

Gabrielson was so interested in Charlie Soong that he arranged to have him honorably discharged after eight months on the *Colfax,* and also arranged for Soong's entrance to Trinity College in Wilmington, North Carolina, a Methodist institution. Charlie converted to Methodism, returned to China and founded a great fortune, becoming the father of the most notable generation of a Chinese family in the history of the country. One of his daughters married Chiang-Kai Shek; another Sun Yat Sen, founder of the Republic of China.

The Lighthouse Service founded a year before the Revenue Marine Service was also a creation of Alexander Hamilton's. On August 7, 1789, the first session of Congress passed an act providing that all expenses

> . . .in the necessary support, maintenance and repairs of all lighthouses, beacons, buoys and public piers erected, placed, or sunk before the passing of this act, at the entrance of, or within any bay, inlet, harbor, or port of the United States, for rendering the navigation thereof easy and safe, shall be defrayed out of the Treasury of United States.[2]

Between 1789 and 1795, all states had ceded their lighthouses to the Federal Government.

This service also came under the jurisdiction of the Treasury Department in its early days. Provisions were made for a keeper and his family, and although his children were not a part of the Lighthouse Service, several interesting incidents involving children, including some girls took their place among the annals of the heroism of the Lighthouse Service. Because the Life-Saving Service was not founded until 1847, many lighthouse keepers doubled as rescuers. If there was a need for additional hands to man the dory in the height of a gale, teenage boys were part of the crew.

Two American girls, daughters of the lighthouse keeper at Scituate, Massachusetts contributed to a repulsion of the British during the War of 1812. In 1814, Rebecca Bates, who was twenty and her sister Abigail only fifteen, were alone at the light-station. Their vantage point provided a view of the harbor where they saw two of the boats from an English warship filled with soldiers move toward a ship in the harbor. They snatched their father's fife and drum, went to the shore and hid behind a bluff where they beat the drum and played the fife as loudly as possible. The crews in the barges upon hearing the martial strains quickly returned to their man-of-war.

Ida Lewis was the daughter of the keeper of Lime Rock Light at Newport, Rhode Island. She began in 1859 at the age of fourteen, to tend the light under the direction of her father, who had been crippled by a stroke. She rescued eleven persons in the following years and upon the death of her father, a special Act of Congress made her keeper of the light. She saved a total of 237 persons before her death fifty years later.

The Lighthouse Service seemed to favor black boys on its lightships. As early as 1838 it was reported by Lieutenant William Porter, U.S. Navy, that when he inspected the Smith's Point Light Boat in the Chesapeake Bay, he found the

> Captain absent, with all of the crew for a week; the boat left in charge of a black boy, fourteen years old; the lantern halfmast, and could not be hoisted by the boy....[3]

In 1887, the Lighthouse Tender *Pansy*, stationed in the Eighth Lighthouse District, listed Nathaniel Lytte as Boy, colored, age fifteen, from Louisiana, who was paid $10 per month and Alphonse Revelle, also colored, and age sixteen, listed as Seaman.

The Life-Saving Service dates back to 1847 officially, but the first life-saver to win fame was Joshua James, who made his first rescue at fifteen in 1843 and remained with the Service until 1902. This youngster was introduced to the savagery of the sea at the age of ten when he saw his brother's schooner tack into Hull Cut near Hull, Massachusetts. His mother and baby sister were aboard and a squall threw the schooner on its beam ends. The ship filled and sank as young Joshua stood sobbing as his mother and sister disappeared. He continued rescuing people until he died at the age of seventy-five as he stepped out of a boat.

The Life Saving Service required its superintendents and keepers to be at least twenty-five and twenty-one respectively, but the surfmen's only requirement was to be able-bodied and experienced. They were paid $40.00 per month in 1877 and $55.00 per month in 1892. They were employed for one year and resided near the station.

In addition, volunteers were paid $10.00 for each saving and they helped to augment the service during the season, which was considered the winter. Six surfmen was average and sometimes eight additional surfmen were hired for the season. It is likely there were teenagers who served as surfmen and volunteers.

The Coast Survey also employed young boys to serve aboard its ships as Wardroom and Cabin Boys. The log book of the Survey Ship *Active* lists a Paul Douglas as a Wardroom Boy, but there is very sketchy information regarding boys in the Survey.

Although these services were quasi-naval, the children who served in them were a part of their history, and contributed their services to the betterment of humanity.

Notes for Chapter 4

1. U.S. Navy Dept. Naval Documents, *Quasi-War* v. II p. 95.
2. George R. Putnam, *Lighthouses & Lights of the United States* (Boston & N.Y.: Houghton, Mifflin, 1917), p. 31.
3. Richard D. White, Jr. "Destination Nowhere: Twilight of the Lightship." *U.S. Naval Institute Proceedings*, March 1976, p. 69.

Crew of U.S. R.C.S. *Seminole* circa 1912 (Boys in background) (Courtesy, United States Coast Guard)

Conclusion

When America went to war in 1917, the apprentice system in the Navy and Marine Corps was nearing its end; the Revenue Cutter Service, the Lighthouse and Lifesaving Services had been absorbed into the U.S. Coast Guard and the U.S. Army has raised its enlistment age to seventeen. Modern warfare had drowned out both drum and bugle; sail had given away to steam.

By 1914, forty-seven states had passed laws which set a minimum age, usually fourteen, for working in industry. These child labor laws, improved economic conditions and educational opportunities brought about the end of the apprentice systems in the armed forces. It was no longer appropriate to have a youngster of fourteen sent away from his family to far away places, to have a drummer of twelve forced to play at funerals or a fifteen-year-old to be a waiter on board ship. The times had changed and the armed forces were forced to change with them.

They had provided a haven for many boys who would otherwise have had no advantages. The services educated them and took them to parts of the world they would never have seen.

Machinery replaced the boys. Purchase and tackle took over for the powder monkey; electronic devices for the drummers and buglers. When World War I called America's patriots to arms, no twelve-year-olds rushed to enlist. Educational progress had reserved a place for them instead of in the ranks. The underaged who managed to don a uniform did so illegally. Twentieth Century warfare required men, not boys; the glamour of the drums and bugles was gone, sail riggings had disappeared. They belonged to another time. Airplanes, gas, submarines and trench warfare had changed the concept of fighting.

America owes a debt to its youthful patriots who served it during good times and bad. The brave young lads who left home and family provided themselves with untold opportunities and brought glory to themselves, their services and their country.

Today's youth should look back to their counterparts of other periods in our history. There they would find lessons of courage, resourcefulness and dedication to duty. They would find that there was a time when the country called its youth to duty and the youth answered the call with honor, courage, and patriotic fervor. The Ponies and Powder Monkeys, the Cadets and Midshipmen, Patriots all, took their place beside their older comrades-in-arms and marched into America's History.

Bibliography

Public Documents

U.S. Congress. House. *Journal.* 3rd Cong. 1st sess. 1793.

———. 3rd Cong. 2nd sess. 1794.

———. *Naval Peace Establishment* No. 56. 9th Cong. 1st sess. 1806.

———. *Laws of the United States in Relation to the Naval Establishment and the Marine Corps* .19th Cong. 1st sess. 1826.

———. *Documents, Legislative and Executive.* 1st Cong. 1st sess.—18th Cong. 2nd sess. (1789-1825). Published 1834.

———. *Laws of the United States in Relation to the Navy and Marine Corps.* 26th Cong. 2nd sess. 1841.

———. Senate. *Medal of Honor Recipients, 1863-1973.* 93rd Cong. 1st sess. 1973. Published 1973.

National Archives. Washington, D.C. Record Group 14—U.S. Navy

Entry 214—Register of Recruits on the Receiving Ship *Ohio*, August 1866-June 1873.

Entry 241—Certificates of Consent for Minors to Enter the Naval Service, 1838-1840.

Entry 242—Certificates of Consent for Minors to Enter the Naval Service, 1867.

Entry 244—Weekly Reports of Boys and Apprentices Received on Board Naval Vessels, 1875-1894.

Entry 248—Descriptive Muster Roll of the Apprentice Ship *Sabine*, July 1864-April 1868.

Entry 249—Returns of Apprentices Enlisted for Duty Aboard the *Sabine*, July 18, 1864-June 22, 1868.
Entry 250—General Record of Naval Apprentices Received Aboard the Apprentice Ship *Sabine*, July 1864-August 1865.
Entry 252—Keys to Enlistment Returns of Boys, 1864-69; 1875-85.
Entry 253—Register of Enlistments of Naval Apprentices 1864-1875.
Entry 360—Composite Shipping Articles of Apprentices on Naval Vessels, 1864-84.
Entry 373—Register of Quarterly Examination of Boys on Board the *Shenandoah*.

________. Record Group 26—U.S. Revenue Cutter Service
Log of Revenue Schooner *Marion*, 1828-1831.
Journal of Revenue Cutters, 1833.
Muster Rolls of Revenue Cutter *Woodbury*, 1837-44.

________. Record Group 94, Records of the Adjutant General's Office, 1782-1917. Memorandum as to Enlistment and Discharge of Minors.

________. Record Group 127—U.S. Marine Corps
Entry 98—Certificates of Indentures, 1814-1856.
Entry 101—Muster Rolls, January 1798-December 1945.
Entry 103—Monthly General Returns of Officers, Non-Commissioned Officers, Musicians and Privates in the Marine Corps, January 1821-February 1903.

________. Record Group 217—Navy Accounts Box 64. Letters from the Secretary of the Navy to Lt. Colonel Commandant Daniel Carmick, 1811. Untitled miscellaneous list.

________. Official Records, The War of the Rebellion
Series 3, V.
Series 1, XVI, part 1.
Series 3, I and II.
Series I, XI, part 1.

________. Enlistment and Indenture Papers—U.S. Army
John Cook, Battery B, 4th U.S. Artillery.
Robert Henderson (Hendershot), 8th Michigan Infantry.
________. U.S.Navy
Jonathan M. Ballard, 2nd Class Boy, 1838.
Hubert M. Bishop, 3rd Class Apprentice, 1888.
John Bishop, 3rd Class Boy, 1863.
________. U.S. Marine Corps
Henry Hooke, Apprentice, 1843.
Lorence Ott, Apprentice, 1847.
John Philip Sousa, Apprentice, 1868.
________. Service records of
Willie Johnston, Musician, Co. D, 3rd Vermont Infantry.
William H. Horsfall, Drummer, Co. G, 1st Kentucky Infantry.
Orion P. Howe, Musician, Co. C, 55th Illinois Infantry.
Nathaniel McL. Gwynne, Private, Troop H, 13th Ohio Cavalry.
John Cook, Bugler, Battery B, 4th U.S. Artillery.
Robinson E.B. Murphy, Musician, Co. A, 127th Illinois Infantry.
James and Allen Thompson, Privates, Co. K, 4th New York Heavy Artillery.
J.C. Julius Langbein, Musician, Co. B, 9th New York Infantry.
Julian A. Scott, Musician, Co. E 34th Vermont Infantry.
Harry Jeremiah Parks, Private, Troop A, 9th New York Cavalry.
Benjamin B. Levy, Musician, Co. G, 1st New York Infantry.
John Lincoln Clem, Co. C, 22nd Michigan Infantry.
Charley Common, Co. A, 52nd Ohio Infantry.
Robert Henry Hendershot, 8th Michigan Infantry.

U.S. Department of the Navy. *Orders and Circulars 1863-1887.*

_______. *Regulations*, 1798, 1800, 1807, 1814, 1832, 1841, 1865, 1876, 1879, 1880, 1896.

_______. *Regulations and Routine of Drills, Exercises and Studies on Board Apprentice-Vessels.* Washington: Government Printing Office, 1859.

_______. Naval Documents *Quasi-War*, v. II, n.d.

U.S. Treasury Department. *Regulations for the U.S. Revenue Cutter Service*, 1834; *Revenue Marine*, 1843; *Revenue Cutter Service*, 1894, 1907, 1915.

_______. *Revised Regulations for the Government of the Life-Saving Services of the U.S., 1877.* Washington: Government Printing Office, 1877.

_______. *Annual Report of the Operations of the U.S. Life-Saving Service for Fiscal Year ending June 30, 1896.* Washington: Government Printing Office, 1897.

_______. *General Orders and Regulations*, 1915.

U.S. War Department. *Regulations of the U.S. Army*, 1813.

_______. *Regulations for the U.S. Military Academy*, 1831, 1839.

_______. *Catalogue of Graduates*, U.S. Military Academy, 1847.

_______. *Revised U.S. Army Regulations of 1861.*

_______. *Regulations for the U.S. Army, 1913 over to 1915.*

Books

Abernathy, Byron R., ed. *Private Elisa Stockwell, Jr. Sees the Civil War.*
Norman: University of Oklahoma Press, 1958.

Ambrose, Stephen E., ed. *A Wisconsin Boy in Dixie: Selected Letters of James K. Newton.* Madison: University of Wisconsin Press, 1961.

Ammen, Daniel. *The Old Navy and the New.* Philadelphia: J.B. Lippincott, 1891.

Aubery, Cullen Bullard. *Recollections of a Newsboy in the Army of the Potomac 1861-1865.* Published by author, 1904.

Bardeen, C.W. *A Little Fifer's Diary*. C.W. Bardeen, 1910.

Bayard, Samuel John. *A Sketch of the Life of Commodore Robert L. Stockton*. New York: Derby & Jackson, 1856.

Bell, Kensil. *Always Ready: The Story of the United States Coast Guard*. New York: Dodd, Mead, 1943.

Benjamin, Park. *The United States Naval Academy*. New York: G.P. Putnam & Sons, 1900.

Benton, Charles Edward. *As Seen from the Ranks: A Boy in the Civil War.* New York: Putnam, 1902.

Bingham, Luther Goodyear. *The Little Drummer Boy*. Boston: Henry Hoyt, 1862.

Bircher, William A. *A Drummer Boy's Diary*. St. Paul: St. Paul Book & Stationery, 1889.

Bixby, William. *Track of the Bear.* New York: David McKay, 1965.

Bloomfield, Howard V.L. *The Compact History of the United States Coast Guard*. New York: Hawthorn Books, 1966.

Bond, O.J. *The Story of the Citadel*. Richmond: Garrett and Massie, 1936.

Buell, Augustus. *History of Andrew Jackson*. New York: Scribner's, 1904.

Burr, Henry L. *Education in the Early Navy* (dissertation). Philadelphia, 1939.

Carse, Robert. *Keepers of the Lights: A History of American Lighthouses.* New York: Charles Scribner's Sons. *1968.*

Clark, H.H. *Boy Life in the United States Navy*. Boston: Lothrop Publishing, 1885.

Cole, Jacob H. *Under Five Commanders or a Boy's Experience with the Army of the Potomac*. Patterson, N.J.: News Printing, 1906.

Collum, Richard S. *History of the United States Marine Corps*. New York: L.R. Hammersly, 1903.

Couper, William. *The V.M.I. New Market Cadets*. Charlottesville, Va.; Michie Co., 1933.

________. *One Hundred Years at V.M.I.* Richmond: Garrett

& Massie, 1939.

Daugherty, Charles V. *Five Years in the Marine Corps*, Vol. 1. Historical Reference Library, U.S.M.C., 1906.

Dewey, George. *Autobiography*. New York: Charles Scribner's Sons, 1913.

Dodge, William Sumner. *Hendershot: Brave Boy of the Rappahannock*. Chicago: Church & Goodman, 1867.

Downey, Fairfax. *Fife, Drum and Bugle*. Fort Collins, Colo.: Old Army Press, 1971.

Drury, Clifford M. *The History of the Chaplain Corps, U.S. Navy Vol. I 1778-1939*. Washington: U.S. Navy Department, 1954.

Eby, Henry Harrison. *Observations of an Illinois Boy in Battle*. Mendota, Ill.: published by author, 1910.

Evans, Stephen H. "The United States Coast Guard 1790-1915." *Annapolis: U.S. Naval Institute*. 1949.

Farragut, Loyal. *The Life of David Glasgow Farragut, Embodying His Journals and Letters*. New York: D. Appleton, 1879.

Figg, Royal W. *Where Men Only Dare To Go*. Richmond: Whittier & Shepperson, 1885.

Forman, Sidney. *West Point*. New York: Columbia University Press, 1950.

Gerry, H.E. *The True History of Robert Henry Hendershot*. Privately printed, n.d.

Greene, Robert Euell. *Black Defenders of America*. Chicago: Johnson Publishing, 1974.

Hall, Harry H. *A Johnny Reb Band from Salem: The Pride of Tarheelia*. Raleigh: the North Carolina Confederate Commission, 1961.

Hartshorn, Edmund F. *Experiences of a Boy by His Father's Son*. Newark: Baker Printing, 1910.

Harwell, Richard Bartsdale. *Confederate Music*. Chapel Hill: University of North Carolina Press, 1950.

Hazen, Jacob. *Five Years Before the Mast*. Philadelphia: W.P. Hazard, 1854.

Heaps, Willard A. *The Bravest Teenage Yanks*. New York: Duell, Sloan and Pearce, 1963.

Heinl, Robert Debs J. *Soldiers of the Sea*. Annapolis: U.S. Naval Institute, 1962.

Hoxse, John. *The Yankee Tar*. Northampton, Mass.: J. Metcalf, 1940.

Hull, Susan Rebecca (Thompson). *Boy Soldiers of the Confederacy*. New York: Neale Publishing, 1905.

Jackson, John W. *The Pennsylvania Navy 1775-1781: The Defense of the Delaware*. New Brunswick: Rutgers University Press, 1974.

Johnson, R.W. *A Soldier's Reminiscences*. Philadelphia: J.B. Lippincott, 1866.

Johnston, David E. *The Story of a Confederate Boy in the Civil War*. Portland: Glass & Prudhomme, 1914.

Karstens, Peter. *The Naval Aristocracy,* Annapolis: U.S. Naval Institute, 1972.

Kieffer, Harry M. *The Recollections of a Drummer Boy of the 150th Pennsylvania Volunteer Regiment, 1883*.

Langley, Harold D. *Social Reform in the United States Navy, 1798-1862*. Urbana: University of Illinois Press, 1967.

Lewis, Charles Lee. *David Glasgow Farragut*. Annapolis: U.S. Naval Institute, 1941.

Lockwood, James D. *Life and Adventures of a Drummer Boy: or Seven Years a Soldier*. Albany: John Skinner, 1893.

Long, David F. *Nothing Too Daring* (biography of Commodore David Porter). Annapolis: U.S. Naval Institute, 1970.

Lord, Francis A. and Arthur Wise. *Bands and Drummer Boys of the Civil War*. New York: Thomas Yoseloff, 1966.

Maclay, Edgar Stanton. *A Youthful Man-O-Warsman*. Greenlawn, N.Y.: Navy Blue Company, 1910.

Mahan, Alfred T. *Admiral Farragut*. New York: D. Appleton, 1897.

Marshall, Edward Chauncey. *History of the U.S. Naval Academy*. New York: D. Van Nostrand, 1862.

Martin, Christopher. *Damn the Torpedoes: The Story of*

America's First Admiral: David Glasgow Farragut. New York: Abelard-Schuman, 1970.

Martin, James Sullivan. *A Narrative of Some of the Adventures, Dangers and Sufferings of a Revolutionary Soldier.* Kennebec, Maine: Glazer, Masters, 1830.

Maury, Dabney. *Recollections of a Virginian.* New York: Charles Scribner's Sons, 1894.

McClellan, Edwin N. *History of the U.S. Marine Corps.* Historical Section, 1925.

McKenzie, Clarence D. *The Little Drummer Boy.* Boston: Henry Hoyt, 1862.

McWhiney, Grady. *Braxton Bragg and the Confederate Defeat.* Vol. I. New York: Columbia University Press, 1969.

Melville, Herman. *White Jacket or The World in a Man-of-War.* Boston: Page, 1892.

Meyers, Augustus. *Ten Years in the Ranks, United States Army.* New York: Stirling Press, 1914.

Miller, Delevan S. *Drum Taps in Dixie: Memories of a Drummer Boy.* Watertown, N.Y.: Hungerford-Holbrook, 1905.

Miller, Trevelyan, ed. *Photographic History of the Civil War.* New York: Review of Reviews, 1912.

Moore, Frank. *The Civil War in Song and Story, 1860-1865.* New York: P.F. Collier, 1889.

Morgan, James Morris. *Confederate Reefer.* Boston: Houghton, Mifflin, 1917.

Nordhoff, Charles. *Nine Years a Sailor: Being Sketches of Personal Experience in the U.S. Naval Service.* Cincinnati: Moore, Wilson & Baldwin, 1866.

________. *Man-of-War Life in the U.S. Navy.* Cincinnati: Moore, Wilstach, Keys, 1856.

Putnam, George R. *Lighthouses and Lightships of the United States.* Boston: Houghton, Mifflin, 1917.

Rand, Edward Augustus. *The Drummer Boy of the Rappahannock: or Taking Sides.* New York: Hunt & Eaton, 1889.

Rauscher, Frank. *Music on the March*. Philadelphia: William F. Fell, 1892.

Rickey, Don Jr. *Forty Miles a Day on Beans and Hay*. Norman: University of Oklahoma Press, 1963.

Robbins, Charles. *The Fife and Drum Instructor*. Exeter, N.H.: C. Norris, 1812.

Samuels, Samuel. *From the Forecastle to the Cabin*. New York: Harper & Brothers, 1887.

Sands, Benjamin F. *From Reefer to Rear Admiral*. New York: Frederick A. Stokes, 1899.

Sheridan P.H. *Personal Memoirs of P.H. Sheridan*. New York: Charles Webster, 1888.

Smith, H.D. *Early History of the United States Revenue Marine*. Washington, D.C.: Naval Historical Foundation, 1932.

Smith, William B. *On Wheels or How I Came There*. New York: Hunt & Eaton, 1892.

Soley, James Russell. *History of the Naval Academy*. Washington: Government Printing Office, 1876.

Stewart, Armistead. *Virginia's Navy of the Revolution*. Richmond: Mitchell and Hotchkiss, 1933.

Story of the Fifty-Fifth Illinois Voluntary Regiment. Clinton, Mass.: Coulter, 1887.

Trowbridge, John T. *The Drummer Boy: A Story of Burnside's Expedition*. Boston: Lee & Shepherd, 1891.

Trowbridge, Silas. *Autobiography*. Vera Cruz: the Trowbridge family, 1872.

Ulmer, George T. *Drummer Boy from Maine*. Chicago: George T. Ulmer, 1892.

Utley, Robert M. *Frontiersmen in Blue*. New York: Macmillan, 1967.

Wells, Tom Henderson. *The Confederate Navy: A Study in Organization*. University: University of Alabama Press, 1971.

West, Richard S. Jr. *The Second Admiral: A Life of David Dixon Porter, 1813-1891*. New York: Coward-McCann, 1937.

Wheeler, Richard. *In Pirate Waters*. New York: Thomas Y. Crowell, 1969.

White, W.C. *A History of Military Music in America*. New York: Exposition Press, 1944.

Wiley, Irvin Bell. *The Life of Billy Yank*. Indianapolis: Bobbs-Merrill, 1951.

_______. *The Life of Johnny Reb*. Indianapolis: Bobbs-Merrill, 1943.

William, T. Harry. *P.G.T. Beauregard*. Baton Rouge: Louisiana State University Press, 1954.

Willison, Charles A. *Reminiscences of a Boy's Service*. Menosha, Wisc.: George Banta, 1908.

Young, Jesse Bowman. *What a Boy Saw in the Army*. New York: Hunt & Eaton, 1894.

Periodicals

Bert, Henry Lawson. "Letters of a Drummer Boy," *Indiana Magazine of History*, 34 (1938): 324-33.

Bryerly, Tate. "A Lad in the War of 1812," *The Researcher*, 1 (1927).

Child, Bert B. "Civil War Musicians," *Annals of Iowa*, 25 (October 1943).

Fletcher, Ebenezer, "Narrative of Captivity," *The Magazine of History*, 38 (1929): 9.

Funk, Arville L., "George Washington's Drummer Boy," *Outdoor Indiana* (February 1964).

Indiana National Guardsman, "Grave of Drummer Boy Discovered," (February 1961).

Quaife, M.M., ed., "A Boy Soldier under Washington: The Memoir of Daniel Gregory," *Mississippi Valley Historical Review*, 16 (March 1930).

Sailor's Magazine & Naval Journal, "A Cabin Boy's Locker," 3, 1830-31.

Shippen Edward. "Some Accounts of the Origin of the Naval Asylum at Philadelphia," Pennsylvania Magazine of History and Biography, 7, 2, (1882).

White, William G. "Martial Music in the U.S. Army," *Recruiting News*, 16 (15 May 1934): 713.

White, Richard D. Jr. "Destination Nowhere: Twilight of the Lightship." *U.S. Naval Institute Proceedings*, (March 1976): 69.

Miscellaneous

Diary of Hugh Roden, Co. K, 7th Regiment, New Jersey Volunteers, September 1861-1864, Clements Library, University of Michigan, Ann Arbor.

Diary of Eben P. Sturges, Adjutant and Aide-de-Camp to John M. Brannon, Commander, Battery M, 1st Ohio Light Artillery Regiment, letter home 12 January 1864. U.S. Military History Research Collection, Carlisle Barracks, Pennsylvania.

Letter, Colonial Richard Delafield, Superintendent, U.S. Military Academy, to Colonel O. Cooper, Adjutant General, U.S. Army, 29 March 1859. U.S. Military Academy Archives.

Index

85-1069
305.2
Bis
Bishop, Eleanor C.
Ponies, patriots
and powder monkeys
DEMCO